CHOCTAW MUSIC

Da Capo Press Music Reprint Series

CHOCTAW MUSIC

By Frances Densmore

DA CAPO PRESS · NEW YORK · 1972

Library of Congress Cataloging in Publication Data

Densmore, Frances, 1867-1957.
  Choctaw music.

  (Da Capo Press music reprint series)
  Reprint of the 1943 ed., which was issued as Anthro-
pological paper 28 of the Bureau of American Ethnology,
p. 101-188 of its Bulletin 136.
  Bibliography: p.
  1. Indians of North America—Music. 2. Choctaw
Indians. I. Title. II. Series: U.S. Bureau of
American Ethnology. Bulletin 136. III. Series:
U.S. Bureau of American Ethnology. Anthropological
papers 28.
ML3557.D3554   784.7'51   72-1883
ISBN 0-306-70511-7

This Da Capo Press edition of *Choctaw Music* is an
unabridged republication of Anthropological Paper 28
of the Bureau of American Ethnology, Smithsonian
Institution, published originally in Washington, D.C.,
in 1943 as pages 101-188 (plates 10–21) of Bulletin 136
of the Bureau of American Ethnology.

Published by Da Capo Press, Inc.
A Subsidiary of Plenum Publishing Corporation
227 West 17th Street, New York, New York 10011

CHOCTAW MUSIC

SMITHSONIAN INSTITUTION
BUREAU OF AMERICAN ETHNOLOGY

Choctaw Music

By FRANCES DENSMORE

Anthropological Papers, No. 28

From Bureau of American Ethnology BULLETIN 136, pp. 101–188, pls. 10–21

UNITED STATES
GOVERNMENT PRINTING OFFICE
WASHINGTON : 1943

SMITHSONIAN INSTITUTION
Bureau of American Ethnology
Bulletin 136

Anthropological Papers, No. 28

Choctaw Music

By FRANCES DENSMORE

FOREWORD

The following study of Choctaw music was conducted in January 1933, as part of a survey of Indian music in the Gulf States, made possible by a grant-in-aid from the National Research Council. A certain peculiarity had been observed in songs of the Yuma of southern Arizona, the Pueblo Indians of New Mexico, the Seminole of Florida, and the Tule Indians of Panama. The purpose of the survey was to ascertain whether this peculiarity was present in the songs of other tribes in the South. This purpose was fulfilled by the discovery of this peculiarity in songs of the Choctaw living near the Choctaw Indian Agency at Philadelphia, Miss. No trace of the peculiarity was found in songs of the Alabama in Texas, and no songs remained among the Chitimacha of Louisiana. On leaving Mississippi, the research was resumed among the Seminole near Lake Okeechobee in Florida. On this extended trip the writer had the helpful companionship of her sister, Margaret Densmore.

The Choctaw represent a group of Indians whose music has not previously been studied by the writer and their songs are valuable for comparison with songs collected in other regions and contained in former publications.[1]

Grateful acknowledgment is made to the National Research Council for the opportunity of making this research.

FRANCES DENSMORE.

---

[1] See bibliography (Densmore, 1910, 1913, 1918, 1922, 1923, 1926, 1928, 1929, 1929 a, 1929 b, 1932, 1932 a, 1936, 1937, 1938, 1939, 1942).

CONTENTS

PAGE

List of songs_____ 107
    1. Arranged in order of serial numbers_____ 107
    2. Arranged in order of catalog numbers_____ 109
Names of singers and number of songs transcribed, exclusive of duplicates_ 111
Characterization of singers and places where songs were recorded_____ 111
Special signs used in transcription of songs_____ 112
Brief list of words used by the Choctaw of Mississippi_____ 112
The Choctaw tribe_____ 115
Musical instruments_____ 117
Certain peculiarities of Choctaw songs_____ 118
War songs_____ 122
Ball game_____ 127
Bullet game_____ 132
Dances_____ 134
    Tick dance_____ 135
    Drunken-man dance_____ 143
    Duck dance_____ 149
    Snake dance_____ 151
    Steal-partner dance_____ 153
    Bear dance_____ 157
    Stomp dance_____ 160
    Terrapin, Quail, Turkey, Chicken, and Pleasure dances_____ 172
Hunting song_____ 176
Songs connected with pastimes_____ 178
Comparison between the analyses of Choctaw songs and the analyses of
    songs recorded in certain other tribes_____ 181
Melodic and rhythmic analysis of songs by serial numbers (tables 1–12)__ 184
Bibliography_____ 188

ILLUSTRATIONS

PLATES

10. 1, Sidney Wesley. 2, Mary Hickman_____ 188
11. 1, Lysander Tubby. 2, Olman Comby_____ 188
12. 1, Maggie Billie in native dress (1933). 2, Maggie Billie's dress and
    apron_____ 188
13. 1, Maggie Billie's bead collar. 2, Maggie Billie's fancy comb_____ 188
14. Choctaw children in native dress (1933)_____ 188
15. 1, Man's head band of pierced silver. 2, Man's bead collar_____ 188
16. 1, Sidney Wesley approaching through the woods. 2, Mary Hick-
    man's house, where songs were recorded_____ 188
17. 1, Robert Henry's house, where songs were recorded. 2, Group at
    Robert Henry's house when songs were recorded_____ 188

PAGE

18. 1, Man's bead necklace.   2, Racket used in ball game.   3, Scrimmage
      in ball game_____   188
19. Bob Henry holding rackets in position for play_____   188
20. 1, Whistle.   2, Robert Henry blowing whistle_____   188
21. 1, Ball used in ball game.   2, Four handkerchiefs folded for use in
      bullet game_____   188

TEXT FIGURES

3. Design on whistle_____   129
4. Robert Henry's personal design on whistle_____   130

LIST OF SONGS

1. ARRANGED IN ORDER OF SERIAL NUMBERS

WAR SONGS

Serial No.		Catalog No.	Page
1. War song		2208	124
2. "Begging for gunpowder" song		2366	125
3. "I am going"		2367	125
4. "Slacker song"		2368	126
5. Victory song		2369	127

SONGS WITH GAMES

6. Song for success in the ball game | | 2263 | 131
(Duplicate of No. 6) | | 2266 | 131
7. Bullet game song (a) | | 2202 | 133
8. Bullet game song (b) | | 2270 | 134
9. Bullet game song (c) | | 2371 | 134

TICK DANCE SONGS

10. Tick dance song (a) | | 2200 | 136
11. Tick dance song (b) | | 2201 | 137
12. Tick dance song (c) | | 2210 | 138
13. Tick dance song (d) | | 2215 | 139
14. Tick dance song (e) | | 2357 | 140
15. Tick dance song (f) | | 2358 | 140
16. Tick dance song (g) | | 2370 | 141
17. Tick dance song (h) | | 2374 | 141
18. Tick dance song (i) | | 2375 | 142
19. Tick dance song (j) | | 2376 | 142
20. Tick dance song (k) | | 2352 | 143

DRUNKEN-MAN DANCE SONGS

21. Drunken-man dance song (a) | | 2355 | 144
22. Drunken-man dance song (b) | | 2363 | 144
23. Drunken-man dance song (c) | | 2364 | 145
24. Drunken-man dance song (d) | | 2365 | 146
25. Drunken-man dance song (e) | | 2379 | 147
26. Drunken-man dance song (f) | | 2380 | 148
27. Drunken-man dance song (g) | | 2381 | 148
28. Drunken-man dance song (h) | | 2382 | 148

DUCK DANCE SONGS

29. Duck dance song (a) | | 2203 | 150
30. Duck dance song (b) | | 2269 | 151

1. ARRANGED IN ORDER OF SERIAL NUMBERS—Continued

SNAKE DANCE SONGS

Serial No.   Catalog No. Page

31. Snake dance song (a)_____ 2204   152
32. Snake dance song (b)_____ 2373   153

STEAL-PARTNER DANCE SONGS

33. Steal-partner dance song (a)_____ 2377   154
34. Steal-partner dance song (b)_____ 2359   154
35. Steal-partner dance song (c)_____ 2378   155
36. Steal-partner dance song (d)_____ 2360   155
37. Steal-partner dance song (e)_____ 2361   155
38. Steal-partner dance song (f)_____ 2362   156
39. Steal-partner dance song (g)_____ 2205   157

BEAR DANCE SONGS

40. Bear dance song (a)_____ 2192   158
41. Bear dance song (b)_____ 2264   158
42. Bear dance song (c)_____ 2267   159
43. Bear dance song (d)_____ 2268   160

STOMP DANCE SONGS

44. Stomp dance song (a)_____ 2194   161
45. Stomp dance song (b)_____ 2195   162
46. Stomp dance song (c)_____ 2196   163
47. Stomp dance song (d)_____ 2197   164
48. Stomp dance song (e)_____ 2198   165
49. Stomp dance song (f)_____ 2199   166
50. Stomp dance song (g)_____ 2211   167
51. Stomp dance song (h)_____ 2216   168
    (Repetition of No. 51)_____ 2216   168
52. Stomp dance song (i)_____ 2271   169
    (Repetition of No. 52)_____ 2271   169
53. Stomp dance song (j)_____ 2372   170
54. Stomp dance song (k)_____ 2354   170
55. Stomp dance song (l)_____ 2353   171
56. Backward-and-forward dance song_____ 2206   171

MISCELLANEOUS DANCE SONGS

57. Terrapin dance song (a)_____ 2207   172
58. Terrapin dance song (b)_____ 2356   173
59. Quail dance song_____ 2265   173
60. Turkey dance song_____ 2209   174
61. Chicken dance song_____ 2193   175
62. Pleasure dance song_____ 2214   176

HUNTING SONG

63. Hunting song_____ 2272   177

SONGS CONNECTED WITH PASTIMES

64. "Rabbit in the garden"_____ 2212   179
65. A dog chases a raccoon_____ 2213   180

2. Arranged in Order of Catalog Numbers

Catalog No.	Title of song	Name of singer	Serial No.	Page
2192	Bear dance song (a)_____	Sidney Wesley_____	40	158
2193	Chicken dance song_____	____do_____	61	175
2194	Stomp dance song (a)_____	____do_____	44	161
2195	Stomp dance song (b)_____	____do_____	45	162
2196	Stomp dance song (c)_____	____do_____	46	163
2197	Stomp dance song (d)_____	____do_____	47	164
2198	Stomp dance song (e)_____	____do_____	48	165
2199	Stomp dance song (f)_____	____do_____	49	166
2200	Tick dance song (a)_____	____do_____	10	136
2201	Tick dance song (b)_____	____do_____	11	137
2202	Bullet game song (a)_____	____do_____	7	133
2203	Duck dance song (a)_____	____do_____	29	150
2204	Snake dance song (a)_____	____do_____	31	151
2205	Steal-partner dance song (g)_____	____do_____	39	157
2206	Backward-and-forward dance song_	____do_____	56	171
2207	Terrapin dance song (a)_____	____do_____	57	172
2208	War song_____	____do_____	1	124
2209	Turkey dance song_____	____do_____	60	174
2210	Tick dance song (c)_____	____do_____	12	138
2211	Stomp dance song (g)_____	____do_____	50	167
2212	"Rabbit in the garden"_____	____do_____	64	179
2213	A dog chases a raccoon_____	____do_____	65	180
2214	Pleasure Dance_____	____do_____	62	176
2215	Tick dance song (d)_____	____do_____	13	139
2216	Stomp dance song (h)_____	____do_____	51	168
	(Repetition of 2216)_____	____do_____	____	168
2263	Song for success in the ball game__	Robert Henry_____	6	131
2264	Bear dance song (b)_____	____do_____	41	158
2265	Quail dance song_____	____do_____	59	173
2266	Duplicate of No. 2263_____	Gus Willis_____	____	131
2267	Bear dance song (c)_____	____do_____	42	159
2268	Bear dance song (d)_____	____do_____	43	160
2269	Duck dance song (b)_____	____do_____	30	151
2270	Bullet game song (b)_____	____do_____	8	134
2271	Stomp dance song (i)_____	____do_____	52	169
	(Repetition of No. 2271)_____	____do_____	____	169
2272	Hunting song_____	Lysander Tubby____	63	177
2352	Tick dance song (k)_____	Olman Comby_____	20	143
2353	Stomp dance song (1)_____	____do_____	55	171
2354	Stomp dance song (k)_____	Robert Henry_____	54	170
2355	Drunken-man dance song (a)_____	____do_____	21	144
2356	Terrapin dance song (b)_____	____do_____	58	173
2357	Tick dance song (e)_____	Lysander Tubby____	14	140
2358	Tick dance song (f)_____	____do_____	15	140
2359	Steal-partner dance song (b)_____	____do_____	34	154
2360	Steal-partner dance song (d)_____	____do_____	36	155
2361	Steal-partner dance song (e)_____	____do_____	37	155

2. ARRANGED IN ORDER OF CATALOG NUMBERS—Continued

Catalog No.	Title of song	Name of singer	Serial No.	Page
2362	Steal-partner dance song (f)_____	Lysander Tubby____	38	156
2363	Drunken-man dance song (b)_____	_____do_____	22	144
2364	Drunken-man dance song (c)_____	_____do_____	23	145
2365	Drunken-man dance song (d)_____	_____do_____	24	146
2366	"Begging for gunpowder" song___	_____do_____	2	125
2367	"I am going"_____	_____do_____	3	125
2368	"Slacker song"_____	_____do_____	4	126
2369	Victory song_____	_____do_____	5	127
2370	Tick dance song (g)_____	_____do_____	16	141
2371	Bullet game song (c)_____	_____do_____	9	134
2372	Stomp dance song (j)_____	_____do_____	53	170
2373	Snake dance song (b)_____	_____do_____	32	153
2374	Tick dance song (h)[1]_____	_____do_____	17	141
2375	Tick dance song (i)[1]_____	_____do_____	18	142
2376	Tick dance song (j)[1]_____	_____do_____	19	142
2377	Steal-partner dance song (a)[1]_____	_____do_____	33	154
2378	Steal-partner dance song (c)[1]_____	_____do_____	35	155
2379	Drunken-man dance song (e)[1]____	_____do_____	25	147
2380	Drunken-man dance song (f)[1]____	_____do_____	26	148
2381	Drunken-man dance song (g)_____	_____do_____	27	148
2382	Drunken-man dance song (h)_____	_____do_____	28	148
2383	Whistle melody_____	Robert Henry_____	_____	130

[1] Gus Willis joined in the singing of this song.

NAMES OF SINGERS AND NUMBER OF SONGS TRANSCRIBED, EXCLUSIVE OF DUPLICATES

Lysander Tubby --- 27
Sidney Wesley [2] --- 25
Robert Henry --- 6
Gus Willis --- 5
Olman Comby --- 2

Total --- 65

CHARACTERIZATION OF SINGERS AND PLACES WHERE SONGS WERE RECORDED

Sidney Wesley [2] (pl. 10, fig. 1) treats the sick by means of herbs. His hair is white and rather long and he called attention to it as an evidence that he is a doctor. The interpreter stated that his hair was purposely disarranged, according to his regular custom. Although commonly known as Doctor Wesley, he has a Choctaw name given him when a child. In explaining his Choctaw name (see p. 112), the interpreter said, "It means that if anything like game is to be killed, the owner of this name kills it himself instead of leaving the work to be done by someone else." His independence and self-reliance are in accord with his name. Wesley was not asked to record his singing with the sick. He said it is "like praying," and that he never heard of prayer to a "spirit-animal," which is customary in certain other tribes. He said, "The chief tells the doctor to help the sick person." Sidney Wesley lives near the Government Day School at Tucker, 7 miles south of Philadelphia, Miss., and his songs were recorded in the house of his neighbor and friend, Mary Hickman [2a] (pl. 10, fig. 2). He was a particularly pleasant man to work with, and his use of English was sufficient for the simpler phases of the work.

Lysander Tubby (pl. 11, fig. 1) is a much younger man than Wesley and learned the Choctaw songs from an older brother. He lives across the road and a short distance from the Pearl River Day School, which is 8 miles west of Philadelphia. Many dances are held in that locality and Tubby is the leader of the singers. A portion of his songs were recorded in the Pearl River School and a portion were recorded in the office of the United States Indian agent at Philadelphia, whose courtesy is gratefully acknowledged.

Robert Henry [2b] (pl. 20, fig. 2) resides in a different part of the reservation, his home being in Bogue Chitto village, about 14 miles northwest of Philadelphia. Henry takes part in the ceremonial ball game and is considered the best authority on the magic connected with it. Songs were recorded in his house, including a song for success in the game, and the playing of the whistles used before and during the game to bring success.

---

[2] Died May 5, 1937.
[2a] Died August 25, 1934.
[2b] Died December 18, 1940.

Gus Willis is a prominent member of the older group in the tribe and lives at Pearl River. Dances are often held at his house and he leads the singing on these occasions. His Choctaw name is Lo'wintc, the meaning of which is not known. In addition to songs that he sang alone, he recorded songs with Lysander Tubby to show the manner in which other singers join the leader of the singing. His songs were recorded at the Pearl River Day School.

Olman Comby (pl. 11, fig. 2) is a native policeman at the agency and is 40 years of age. He acted as interpreter throughout the work and recorded a limited number of songs at the agency office, when Lysander Tubby's songs were being recorded. He also supplied information on various tribal customs.

SPECIAL SIGNS USED IN TRANSCRIPTION OF SONGS

⌐‾‾‾‾⌐ placed above a series of notes indicates that they constitute a rhythmic unit.

+ placed above a note indicates that the tone is sung slightly less than a semitone higher than the diatonic pitch, in all renditions of the song.

— placed above a note indicates that the tone is sung slightly less than a semitone lower than the diatonic pitch, in all renditions of the song.

.) placed above a note or rest shows that the tone or rest is given less than the indicated time.

BRIEF LIST OF WORDS USED BY THE CHOCTAW OF MISSISSIPPI

These words were noted down as pronounced by the Indians. The corrected spelling and the analysis of doubtful words were supplied by Dr. John R. Swanton, whose cooperation is gratefully acknowledged. The cross ł (the Polish l) is a surd *l*, which approximates English *thl* and is sometimes so rendered.

NAMES OF PERSONS

American name	Indian name	Meaning
Sidney Wesley___	Lapĭn'tabe'se'ihoke'_	Commonly translated, "Kills it himself." This word has in it Ilapintabi, perhaps with the suffix -achi, which may mean "he himself killed it." Ihoke' seems to mean "it is so," hoke being a form of oke from which some think our O. K. is derived. This word is not entirely clear.
Mary Hickman___	Ato' baa' ntci_____	Commonly translated, "putting it back." It may be itabanchi or itabananchi, "to put together," or it may contain atoba, "to make of," or "where a thing is made," and anchi, "to put a robe on."

Musical Instruments

O'skula _____ Whistle.

Ałepa chito _____ Big drum.

Itł' mobûbe' (may be Itimaboa also pronounced
   Itimola be) _____ "Striking things together."
                                              striking sticks.

Dances

Hiła _____ A dance, or "to dance."

Hiła tolupli _____ Stomp dance.

Shatanni hiła _____ Tick dance.

Tinsanałe hiła (perhaps from Choctaw iti^n
   shanąli, to turn or twist around one another) __ Drunken-man dance.

Sinti hiła _____ Snake dance.

Kofi hiła _____ Quail dance.

Itimolevi (should perhaps be Itimilaueli) _____ Steal-partner dance.

Taloa _____ Song.

CHOCTAW MUSIC

By FRANCES DENSMORE

THE CHOCTAW TRIBE

The earliest mention of the Choctaw tribe is in the De Soto narratives.[3] In his march down the Alabama Valley in 1540, De Soto took captive "the giant Tascalusa," chief of the Mobile tribe, which was closely related to the Choctaw. Later he passed through some of the eastern towns of the Choctaw Indians on the Black Warrior River.

The Choctaw are a Muskhogean tribe whose early home was in southeastern Mississippi and southwestern Alabama. They were mainly an agricultural people when the white man came, and their wars were usually defensive.

The French entered this region at the very end of the seventeenth century and established colonies at Mobile, Biloxi, and New Orleans. Concerning the population of the Choctaw tribe, Dr. J. R. Swanton (1922, pp. 450, 451, 454) says, "It would seem from the figures given us by travelers and officials that during the eighteenth century the tribe had a population of about 15,000."

Friendly relations with the French were established and the Choctaw helped the French in their wars on other tribes. In the war against the Natchez in 1730, a large body of Choctaw warriors served under a French officer. This friendly relationship continued until the English traders succeeded in winning some of the eastern Choctaw villages. War followed between the Choctaw who were friendly to the English and those who remained loyal to the French, this war continuing until 1763. In that year, the French surrendered their possessions in the United States to Great Britain, and members of the Choctaw tribe continued to move across the Mississippi River into Louisiana.

The English authorities in the southern colonies made two or three treaties with Indians in that region, fixing boundaries that were

---

[3] For material regarding the social and ceremonial life of the Choctaws, including salient facts of their history, see Swanton (1922, 1931).

referred to in treaties made later with the United States. The first of these is "a treaty between Great Britain and the Chickasaw and Choctaw Indians," made at Mobile, March 26, 1765. Article 5 of this treaty is, in part,

to prevent all disputes on account of encroachments, or supposed encroachments, committed by the English inhabitants of this or any other of His Majesty's Provinces, on the lands or hunting grounds reserved and claimed by the Chickasaw and Choctaw Indians, and that no mistakes, doubts or disputes, may, for the future, arise thereupon, in consideration of the great marks of friendship, benevolence and clemency, extended to us, the said Chickasaw and Choctaw Indians, by His Majesty King George the Third, we, the chiefs and head warriors, distinguished by great and small medals, and gorgets, and bearing His Majesty's commissions as Chiefs and leaders of our respective nations . . . do hereby agree, that, for the future, the boundary be settled by a line extended from Gross Point, in the island of Mount Louis . . . to the mouth of the eastern branch of the Tombecbee River . . .

The exact boundaries are apart from present interest, but the article closes with the statement that "none of His Majesty's subjects shall be permitted to settle on Tombechee River to the northward of the rivulet called Centebonck" (Thomas *in* Royce, 1899, pp. 559, 560).

The first treaty between the Government of the United States and the Choctaw Indians was concluded at Hopewell, S. C., January 3, 1786 (Royce 1899, p. 650). By this treaty the boundaries of certain lands were designated, "the Choctaw nation to live and hunt" within these boundaries. More important was the famous treaty of Dancing Rabbit Creek, September 27–28, 1830, by which all Choctaw, except those who chose to become citizens of the United States, were to surrender their lands east of the Mississippi and to accept in place of them a new Reservation in what is now the State of Oklahoma. The greater part removed soon afterward, but a considerable body, the "Mississippi Choctaw," refused to emigrate, and their descendants remain in their old country to the present day.

The Mississippi Choctaw numbered 2,255 in 1904, 1,162 in 1910, and 1,253 in 1916–19. Harvey K. Meyer, superintendent of the Choctaw Indian Agency at Philadelphia, Miss., states (correspondence December 21, 1939): "When the census for this jurisdiction was compiled in January of the calendar year, a total of 1,974 were then enrolled as eligible Choctaws."

At the present time (1933), many of the Choctaw continue to wear a distinctive costume, evidently influenced by early white settlers. Maggie Billie (pl. 12, fig. 1) is an expert basket maker, and wears this costume when she comes to town. Her dress, apron, woven bead collar, and fancy comb are shown in plates 12 and 13. The latter is made from an ordinary "round comb"; the white ornamentation is cut from a man's celluloid collar and the beadwork is on a stiffened band of dark cloth. The costume of little girls is similar to that of the women (pl. 14). A head band of pierced silver was formerly worn by the men (pl. 15, fig. 1). At present (1933), the typical costume of a man includes a white shirt opened in the back and having a white bosom that is round at the lower edge. With this is worn a flat collar of woven beadwork (pl. 15, fig. 2) and a necklace consisting of many strings of small beads (pl. 18, fig. 1).

MUSICAL INSTRUMENTS

Striking sticks.—The only instrument used by the Mississippi Choctaw in accompanying their songs is a pair of striking sticks. These are made when needed, and those made by Sidney Wesley were about 10 inches long. The sticks are not round, but slightly flattened on two sides, affording suitable surfaces for striking together. This form of percussion is not common among the Indians but was noted among the Menominee in connection with "magic power." [4]

Drum.—Each medicine man at a ball game carried a drum, beating upon it during the game. Robert Henry, Sidney Wesley, and Gus Willis said that, within their knowledge, the drum has been used at no other time by the Mississippi Choctaw. The instrument is a small hand drum. Evidently this was in general use at an earlier time, as a missionary wrote, "The ancient Choctaw, in all his solemn ceremonies, as well as amusements and merrymakings, did not depend upon the jarring tones of the diminutive drum as he did upon his own voice" (Cushman, 1899). The same authority mentions a drum made from the trunk of a tree.

The Choctaw at Bayou Lacomb, La., used a drum made from a tree trunk.[5]

Whistles.—A description of the cane whistles used by the Choctaw is contained in the section on the ball game (pp. 129, 130). These were blown by the medicine men on the night before that game, and during

---

[4] David Amab described the opening of his grandfather's "medicine bundle" at a feast to secure success in hunting. "Amab helped his grandfather prepare the sticks which were tapped together during the songs . . . Those made for the writer were about 9 inches long, but it was not unusual for a hunter to use sticks that were longer. One stick was designated as the 'beater,' and a song concerning this stick was recorded, with the sticks tapped together as an accompaniment" (Densmore, 1932, p. 65).

[5] "The only musical instrument known to the Choctaw of Bayou Lacomb is the drum (the'ba) a good example of which is represented in plate 7. This is 30 inches in height and 15 inches in diameter. It is made of a section of a black gum tree; the cylinder wall is less than 2 inches in thickness. The head consists of a piece of untanned goat skin. The skin is stretched over the open end, while wet and pliable, and is passed around a hoop made of hickory about half an inch thick. A similar hoop is placed above the first. To the second hoop are attached four narrow strips of rawhide, each of which is fastened to a peg passing diagonally through the wall of the drum. To tighten the head of the drum it is necessary merely to drive the peg farther in. In this respect, as well as in general form, the drum resembles a specimen from Virginia in the British Museum, as well as the drum even now in use on the west coast of Africa. It is not possible to say whether this instrument is a purely American form or whether it shows the influence of the Negro." (Bushnell, 1909, p.22.) This is similar to the "voodoo drum" of Haiti, a notable example of which is in the United States National Museum. (Cf. Densmore, 1927, p. 57, pl. 23, c.)

the game to bring success to certain groups of players. No other use of the instrument was mentioned by the informants.

CERTAIN PECULIARITIES OF CHOCTAW SONGS

Period formation.—A definite form consisting of several periods, recurring in regular order, was first noted by the writer when recording songs of the Yuma Indians, in 1922 (Densmore, 1932). This observation led, eventually, to the study of Choctaw songs in which the same peculiarity was found. The periods, or sections, in these songs are of relative lengths, the second period being much shorter than the first, also higher in pitch and different in rhythm. The first period is usually repeated, but the second is rarely repeated and is followed by a recurrence of the first period, or by one or two other periods. In transcription, these are indicated by the letters A, B, C, and D.

The "period formation" was found, in a somewhat modified form, in songs of the Tule Indians from San Blas, Panama, recorded in Washington in 1924 (Densmore, 1926), and occurred with marked frequency in the songs from Santo Domingo Pueblo, N. Mex. (Densmore, 1938),[6] and in the songs from Acoma, Isleta, and Cochiti Pueblos.[7] No evidence of it was found in Nootka and Quileute songs (Densmore, 1939), nor in songs recorded in British Columbia (Anthrop. Pap. No. 27) and in many tribes of Indians in the United States. It was, however, found in a few of the oldest songs recorded among the Seminole Indians in Florida.[7] Under these circumstances, it seemed desirable to ascertain the distribution of the peculiarity among Indians in the Gulf States. Such a survey was made possible by a grant from the National Research Council and the work began in December 1932. The first tribe visited was the Alabama in Texas. Sixty-two songs were recorded, but none contained this form. The Chitimacha of Louisiana were selected as the next tribe for observation (Densmore, 1943), but no songs remained in that tribe. The oldest man related stories in which songs were formerly sung, but said that he "never was a singer and did not learn the songs."

The Choctaw living near the Choctaw Indian Agency at Philadelphia were then visited and, as usual, the work was begun with the oldest medicine man in the group. Sidney Wesley was asked to record the oldest songs that he could remember, and the period formation was heard in his first song (No. 61). He was encouraged to remember other old songs and the period formation was heard in the fourth, fifth, seventh, eighth, and eleventh songs that he recorded,

---

[6] Pages 51 and 52 state that, from the records, this "appears to have been an early custom in Mexico . . . at the time of the Conquest."

[7] Unpublished material, Bureau of American Ethnology.

as well as in four subsequent recordings.   Thus the period formation occurred in 10 of the 25 songs recorded by the oldest Choctaw singer. Next to Wesley in seniority was Robert Henry, who recorded 6 songs, one of which contained the period formation.   This did not occur in 27 dance songs recorded by Lysander Tubby and 2 songs recorded by Olman Comby, both being younger singers who recorded only the songs of various dances.

Two periods, designated as A and B, occur in Nos. 11, 12, 40, 41, 45, 46, 48, 49, 51, and 60, and three periods, designated as A, B, and C, in Nos. 56 and 61.

Absence of instrumental accompaniment in certain songs.—This custom was mentioned by informants and noted at the dance attended at Pearl River.   The dances without instrumental accompaniment, according to informants, are the War, Tick, Drunken-man, Snake, Steal-partner, and Stomp dances; the songs of the bullet game are also without accompaniment.   When listening to the songs at the dance, an effort was made to explain the precision and rhythm without accompaniment.   The explanation was found in the manner of singing the songs, especially by the leader.   The rhythm was emphasized vocally, and the structure of the melody contributed to the effect.   The former peculiarity was afterward heard in the unaccompanied singing of a chorus of Negroes.   There was the same throb of a fundamental tone, producing a rhythmic effect not unlike that of an accompanying instrument.   Mention may be made here of another mannerism common to Choctaw and Negro singing.   This consists in the occasional use of the labial *m*, produced with the lips closed and continuing for the duration of a sixteenth to a dotted quarter note.   This was heard also in a few Seminole songs recorded in Florida and in songs of a Makah medicine man, recorded at Neah Bay, Wash., where a company of Spaniards lived for a short time. The Makah singer said this visit of the Spaniards took place during the life of his grandfather's grandfather.   The use of the labial may have occurred in the singing of men connected with this expedition, and the Indians may have adopted it, thinking the peculiar sound was connected with "medicine power."   This would be in accord with Indian custom.   The labial is transcribed with five Makah songs, all being connected with dreams and two being used in the treatment of the sick (Densmore, 1939, pp. 149, 150, 177, 178).   The labial in Choctaw singing appears to be without significance, and is not indicated in the transcriptions.

The melodic structure of the Choctaw dance songs is marked by an unusual number of recurrent tones and intervals.   The recurrent tone is usually the lowest tone of the melody and its repetition gives a rhythmic effect, like the stroke of a percussion instrument.   In

other songs, a recurring interval is followed by a short rest, giving
it prominence. This peculiarity cannot be shown in the transcription, but was clearly heard in the repetitions of the songs, at the
dance at Pearl River. Examples of songs with recurring tones are
Nos. 10, 11, 14, 15, 16, and 17 in the Tick dance songs, No. 37 in the
Steal-partner dance songs, and Nos. 45 and 48 in the Stomp dance
songs. Examples of songs with recurrent descending intervals are
the Snake dance songs (Nos. 31, 32) and the Stomp dance songs No.
46 and Nos. 50.to 54. Thus the leader of the Choctaw singers had
a responsibility beyond the actual leading of the songs. He inter-
preted them by his rendition in such a manner that an accompanying
instrument was not necessary.

Striking sticks used as percussion accompaniment.—Indian singers
in other tribes have desired some form of percussion accompaniment
when recording their songs. The sound of an Indian drum does
not record clearly and various substitutes have been used, such as
pounding on a pasteboard box, the resultant sound having definite-
ness without resonance. A Makah singer preferred to pound on the
floor with a cane, this sound being clearly recorded. The Choctaw
singers did not care for any support to the voice and used the striking
sticks only in songs with which they would be used at public gather-
ings. An exception is the duplicate of the song for success at a
ball game (Duplicate of No. 6). This was the first song recorded by
Willis, who had not been questioned closely on tribal customs.
Lysander Tubby had been recording songs and the striking sticks
were in the room, so Willis used them with this first recording.

The striking sticks are described and their use by the Menominee
is mentioned on page 117. This form of accompaniment was used
with the Bear, Quail, Duck, Terrapin, Turkey, Chicken, and Pleasure
dances. (See table 12, p. 187.)

Different "shouts" with each class of dance songs.—These vocalizations, somewhat resembling yells, were rhythmic and preceded and
followed the singing of the songs. The leader of the singers began
these and the others joined him. The tone was not a singing tone
and the shouts cannot be transcribed with any degree of accuracy in
musical notation. Two types of these shouts are shown as nearly as
is possible in notation, these being the shouts that preceded the Bear
dance (No. 42) and those that followed the recording of a Snake dance
song (No. 32). This custom has not been observed in northern tribes,
though various sorts of yells and vocalizations often precede or follow
Indian songs, or may occur during songs at a dance. It may be a
form of the "hollering," which is a custom in Negro singing and was
designated by that name among the Seminole of Florida.

Swaying effect in melodies of many dance songs.—The rhythmic effect of a dance song is generally due to the spacing of accents and the divisions of the counts, but in many Choctaw dance songs a swaying, rhythmic effect is produced by an alternation of ascending and descending, or descending and ascending intervals. This sequence is repeated throughout the song, and the effect is increased by the repetitions of the song. Among the examples of this rhythmic effect are Nos. 11, 13, 14, 16, 19, 23, 24, 31, 39, 40, 42, 43, and 51.

Indeterminate ending.—The renditions of 2 Choctaw dance songs (Nos. 18 and 19) end on the tone above the keynote. This peculiarity was observed first in a dance song of the Cocopa Indians, living near the southern border of Arizona (Densmore, 1932, song No. 111, p. 182). It was observed next in 8 songs of the Nootka and Quileute in northwestern Washington,[8] and has been found in a few Seminole songs. A tabulated analysis of 1,553 songs recorded among widely separated tribes of Indians shows these 9 songs ending on the second, 1 ending on the sixth, 71 regarded as irregular (without apparent keynote), and the remainder ending on a tone having a chord-relationship to the keynote.

No explanation has been offered for the ending of songs on the tone above the keynote in other tribes, but we note that the duration of certain dances among the Choctaw was said to be the time of dancing around the circle. This would terminate the song arbitrarily. An Indian believed to have been a Choctaw said, "the singing can stop at any time." In view of these circumstances, the ending of a rendition on the tone above the keynote is regarded as an indeterminate ending. It is as though the singer wished to indicate that the singing could be continued through other renditions of the song.

A second voice recorded.—At the suggestion of Lysander Tubby, a second voice, or "part," was recorded with a few of his songs to show the manner in which other voices join that of the leader. Gus Willis was present and consented to sing this "second part," beginning after Tubby and continuing in unison with him. The songs in which he sang with Tubby are Nos. 17, 18, 19, 25, 26, 33, and 35. His voice blended with Tubby's so completely that his entrance could not be discerned on the phonograph record, but notes were made during the performance, stating that Willis entered on the fourth measure in No. 17 and at about the same point in the other songs. During the performance of No. 33, Willis omitted certain single tones, Tubby's voice being heard alone on those tones. Willis also sang the long

---

[8] Densmore, 1932, Tabulated analysis, p. 36. The Nootka songs with this ending are Nos. 10, 19, and 20, songs of the potlatch; Nos. 44 and 45, songs of the lightning dance with the Klokali; No. 103, a war song; and No. 172, a Clayoquot song to calm the waves of the sea. The Quileute song is No. 200, used in the treatment of the sick.

tones in this song with a vibrato. From this it appears that the second voice may vary its performance without changing the melody. Willis, as stated, has been a leader of the singers at dances and is considered an authority on the old musical customs.

WAR SONGS

The oldest song [9] in the present collection is probably the war song recorded by Sidney Wesley. In order to contact this interesting man, the writer went to his house, but he was not at home. The house was difficult to reach, and it was necessary to leave the car, walk through a ravine, and climb a hill on the opposite side. His house was closed, evidently having been unoccupied for some time. Returning to the car, Olman Comby, the interpreter, looked up the valley, and exclaimed, "There comes Wesley." A man was seen at a considerable distance, making his way among the bushes and carrying a pack on his back and a large pail in one hand. As he came nearer, his white hair could be seen, blown back from his face. When he was within hailing distance, Comby called to him and, instead of going up the hill to his house, he crossed the ravine to where we were standing. Evidently he was disturbed about something, which he tried to explain in broken English. This failing, he changed to his native language and told the policeman that he had been trying to live with his daughter but she "would not control her children nor let him reprove them," so he was going back to live alone in his own little house.

After this had been duly discussed, the matter of recording old songs was explained and he consented to sing, suggesting that the recording be done at the home of Mary Hickman, an active old woman living alone, near the Tucker Day School. An arrangement was made with her and the work began on the following day. In plate 16, figure 1, Wesley is seen approaching Mary Hickman's house, bringing a pair of striking sticks, which he has made for use as an accompaniment to his songs.

Mary Hickman is familiar with all the old ways. Her house (pl. 16, fig. 2) has no windows and is warmed by a fireplace. The phonograph was placed on a bench just inside the door and she sat on the porch with her sewing, where she could hear and see all that was said or done, and occasionally she was consulted by Wesley or the interpreter. The house was neat and quiet and the place, with its surroundings of tall pines, was admirably adapted to the work. The open door of the house is seen in the background of her portrait and

---

[9] These songs were recorded by Columbia gramophone with special recorders and a specially constructed horn. The speed of the apparatus when recording the songs and when playing them for transcription was 160 revolutions per minute.

that of Wesley (pl. 10, figs. 1 and 2). Thirty songs were recorded by Wesley, 25 of which were transcribed. He selected the songs himself and gave an agreeable variety, which included songs of games, pastimes, and dances, as well as the war song which opens the series.

Sidney Wesley and Mary Hickman danced in the war dances when they were young. There were no wars at that time, but the war dances were held and some of the old songs were sung on those occasions.

Two records of the first song were made, one containing the words "Hispanimi (Spanish) headman I am looking for," and the other substituting "Folance" (French) for the reference to the Spaniards. Wesley did not know the meaning of either of these words, but sang the song as he learned it. The song had two more "verses," each containing the name of a different enemy. One verse mentioned a tribe of Indians that was not identified. A portion of the native name was said to mean horsefly, which was probably a term of contempt. The underscored syllables in the transcription are probably parts of words whose meaning is lost. Both men and women sang in the war dances, and the songs were without instrumental accompaniment.

The contact of the Choctaw with the Spanish, as stated, began about 1540. The French entered the region in the latter part of the seventeenth century and the relations between the Choctaw and the French were friendly until broken by English traders. The eastern Choctaw villages formed an alliance with the English, and war ensued between them and the Choctaw toward the west, who still adhered to the French. From this data it appears that the song originated with the Choctaw in Mississippi and that it is very old.

No. 1. War Song

Recorded by SIDNEY WESLEY

(Catalog No. 2208)

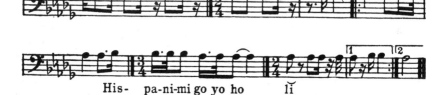

His- pa-ni-mi go yo ho li

Analysis.[10]—This melody is based on intervals, not on the relationship of tones to a keynote. The principal interval is a whole tone. occurring chiefly between A flat and B flat, next in frequency being the minor third between B flat and D flat. The keynote is regarded as D flat, which occurs as next to the highest tone, and the melody contains only this tone with its second and fifth.

A group of four war songs was recorded by a man who learned them from an older brother. It was said that the first song was sung at the beginning of the preparations for war. No explanation could be obtained beyond the purpose suggested by the title.

---

[10] These analyses are intended to call attention only to the principal peculiarities of the songs. More detailed descriptive analyses, as well as tabulated analyses, have been submitted to the Bureau of American Ethnology. Small variations in repetitions of songs, if unimportant, are not mentioned in these analyses. The Choctaw singers, like the singers in other tribes, usually sing the major third, perfect fifth, and octave with good intonation, whether as direct or indirect (broken) intervals, and usually maintain the pitch level of a song throughout the renditions. The semitone is the most variable progression in Indian songs.

No. 2. "Begging for Gunpowder" Song

(Catalog No. 2366)

Recorded by LYSANDER TUBBY

Analysis.—A descending fourth followed by an ascending fourth characterizes this song, which is minor in tonality, with the keynote occurring as the highest tone of the compass.

In the next song a man expresses his willingness to go with the war party and his confidence in his protective "medicine."

No. 3. "I Am Going"

(Catalog No. 2367)

Recorded by LYSANDER TUBBY

Free translation

I am going. (Repeated many times.)
My face is painted so they cannot see me.

Analysis.—This interesting melody is based on the minor triad and minor seventh, with the tones occurring in descending order. Slight differences in the repetitions are shown, these occurring in the middle of the song, where changes most frequently occur in the melodic or rhythmic pattern of an Indian song. The transcription is a semitone lower than the pitch of the rendition. As in similar instances, a simpler signature is used when the pitch of the rendition would require six sharps or flats.

Indians of all tribes ridiculed the men who would not go to war. The next song concerns two men who are arranging to run away and evade their duty. One man was to go ahead and wait for the other at an appointed place, after which they would proceed together. The title was given by the singer.

No. 4. "Slacker Song"

(Catalog No. 2368)

Recorded by LYSANDER TUBBY

Free translation

I will tell you how we are going.
When you get to that place you must wait for me.

Analysis.—As in No. 2, the keynote occurs only as the highest tone in this melody. The peculiar measure lengths were accurately repeated in all the renditions, also the length of the rests. This transcription contains a plus sign over several notes, showing the tone was slightly above the indicated pitch. This occurs also in Nos. 5, 22, 23, 25, 28, 36, and 38, and is used only when the deviation from pitch is persistent in all the renditions.

The final song of the group celebrates a victory.

No. 5. Victory Song

Recorded by Lysander Tubby

(Catalog No. 2369)

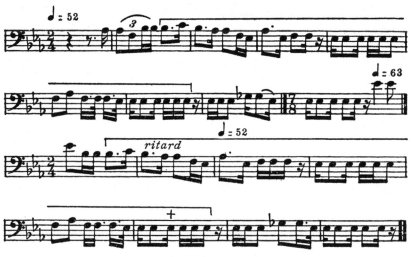

Free translation

Where I went along they saw my tracks,
After I killed him they saw my tracks and cried.
My headman told men to kill him,
I killed him because my headman told me to,
I hid in the bushes after killing him, but they came near seeing me.

Analysis.—In contrast to the preceding war songs, the keynote of this melody is the lowest tone and is strongly emphasized. This gives an effect of positiveness that has been noted in songs of success in other tribes. A change to minor tonality is indicated by an accidental rather than by a change of signature.

BALL GAME

The playing of the ball game by the Choctaw is a contest of magic power as well as a contest of skill.[11]   Each group of players has its own medicine men who perform various acts to bring success to them and disaster to their opponents. These men are designated by a word commonly translated "witches," but they will be referred to as medicine men.

---

[11] "In general, in all Indian games, the arrow or the bow, or some derivative of them, is found to be the predominant implement, and the conceptions of the four world-quarters the fundamental idea . . .   Back of each game is found a ceremony in which the game was a significant part. The ceremony has commonly disappeared; the game survives as an amusement, but often with traditions and observances which serve to connect it with its original purpose. The ceremonies appear to have been to cure sickness, to cause fertilization and reproduction of plants and animals, and, in the arid region, to produce rain . . .   These observations hold true both of the athletic games as well as of the games of chance. The ball was a sacred object not to be touched with the hand, and has been identified as symbolizing the earth, the sun, or the moon" (Culin *in* Handbook of American Indians, 1907, vol. 1, p. 484).

Two men were consulted on this subject. They are considered authorities on the game and live in different localities. Robert Henry lives at Bogue Chitto village and was consulted in his home (pl. 17, fig. 1), and Gus Willis lives at Pearl River. Both men recorded the song that is sung the night before a game, and a comparison of the two renditions is presented with the analysis of the song on page 131. Robert Henry also recorded the sounds of the whistles that are played before and during a game (see p. 129; also Whistle Melody, p. 130). The group at Henry's house included Olman Comby, the interpreter (center), Robert Henry (at his left), members of Henry's family, and informants on the action of the ball game (pl. 17, fig. 2).

Five or six medicine men were attached to each team of players, in former times, and each medicine man had two or three whistles, a drum, and a wand with some small object at the tip. Robert Henry remembered such a wand as having what looked like a red bird at its end. Its use was not described. The whistles are still used and are of different lengths, each having a different mark on one side.

Each player has his own rackets, which are "fixed up" by the medicine men to give success. In old days, the balls were made by the medicine men. It was said, "Some could make a ball that was sure to go straight," and a player would pay a medicine man to make such a ball. This custom has passed away and at present a ball has an ordinary rubber ball as its core. A pair of rackets and a ball were transferred to the writer and are in the possession of the United States National Museum. The ball is covered with a lattice of narrow strips of buckskin. (Pls. 18, fig. 2; 21, fig. 1.)

Before a game the players lay their rackets on the ground and one of their medicine men inspects them. Both Robert Henry and Olman Comby saw this done by an old man named Silwis. A medicine man may put "good medicine" on the rackets of his team of players, and he watches for a chance to put "bad medicine" on the rackets of the opponents, so their balls will "go crooked." A medicine man attached to one side may go to the goal posts of the opponents and "spoil their game," so it is part of the duty of the medicine men to keep the opposing medicine men from coming near their goal posts.

On the night before a ball game, the whistles are blown by the medicine men, there is "talking" in which it is asserted that "You are going to win the game," and the song for success is sung. The whistles are blown during a game, and the medicine men beat on their drums, but there is no singing while the game is in progress. The sound of the whistles during a game was referred to as "the noise made by the witches."

One of the medicine men gives the signal for beginning the game. Each has a ball of a different color and one of them is appointed to give the signal, which he does by tossing up his ball. The players hold a racket in each hand and are not allowed to touch the ball with their hands. Bob Henry posed with the crossed rackets (pl. 19). Three young Choctaw posed a "scrimmage" in the game (pl. 18, fig. 3). The purpose, as in similar ball games, is to throw the ball between the opponent's goal posts.[12] The details of the play and its score are not of present interest. During a game, the medicine men take turns in standing near the goal posts of their respective teams, to prevent the approach of the opposing medicine men who, it is believed, will cause disaster by means of evil magic.

Figure 3.—Design on whistle.

The blowing of cane whistles by the medicine men before and during a ball game has been mentioned. Robert Henry has three of these whistles, which he is accustomed to use at the game, and he recorded the sound of each, playing one after another in rapid succession. Each whistle had its special marking. The first was 12½ inches in length and etched (burned) with the design shown in figure 3. The

[12] "The [racket] game may be divided into two principal classes—first, those in which a single racket or bat is used; second, those in which two rackets are employed. The latter is peculiar to the southern tribes (Cherokee, Choctaw, Muskogee, Seminole), among whom the single racket is not recorded . . . The goals were commonly two sets of posts or poles erected at the extremities of the field, between which the ball had to be driven . . . Among the Choctaw the goals were connected by a pole at the top." (Culin, 1907, pp. 562, 563.)

A variation of this game among the Choctaw of Louisiana was witnessed by Bushnell in 1909 and described by him. "No rackets were used, the ball being caught in the hands and thrown or held while the player endeavored to reach his opponent's goal." (Bushnell, 1909, p. 20.)

second is shown in plate 20, figure 1, and is in the possession of the United States National Museum. This and the third whistle were 11 inches in length. The third whistle was etched with Robert Henry's personal mark (fig. 4). The performance on the second whistle was transcribed, the others being studied and found to contain the same melody. The pitch of the first whistle was a semitone lower than the

FIGURE 4.—Robert Henry's personal design on whistle.

transcription. The pitch of the third was a whole tone higher than the transcription. The length of the whistle was the same, but the fingerholes were spaced differently. As shown in the portrait of Robert Henry blowing the whistle (pl. 20, fig. 2), the first finger of each hand was placed over a sound hole, the middle finger of the player's left hand being placed between the two sound holes.

Whistle Melody

(Catalog No. 2383)

Recorded by ROBERT HENRY

The song that was sung the night before a ball game, to give success to the players, was recorded by two men.

No. 6. Song for Success in the Ball Game

(Catalog No. 2263)

Recorded by ROBERT HENRY

Duplicate of No. 6

(Catalog No. 2266)

Recorded by GUS WILLIS

Voice ♩ = 60
Striking sticks ♩ = 60
See rhythm of striking sticks below

Rhythm of striking sticks

Analysis.—This melody is almost an incantation, in its simplicity of melody and rhythm. Two renditions are presented, each by a man regarded as an authority on the ball game. The essential rhythm and melody are the same, with a variation that seems permissible among the Choctaw. In both renditions the only descending progressions are whole tones. Both renditions have a compass of a major third. Frequent rests occur in the rendition by Henry, dividing the melody into phrases, but the rendition by Willis, lasting 20 seconds, was sung without a pause for breath.

The events of the night before a ball game included dancing by both men and women. This is described as follows by Catlin (1913, vol. 2, pp. 142, 143) :

The ground having been all prepared and preliminaries of the game all settled, and the bettings all made, and goods all "staked," night came on without the appearance of any players on the ground. But soon after dark, a procession of lighted flambeaux was seen coming from each encampment, to the ground where the players assembled around their respective byes; and at the beat of the drums and chants of the women, each party of players commenced the "ball-play dance." Each party danced for a quarter of an hour around their respective byes, in their ball-play dress; rattling their ball sticks together in the most violent manner, and all singing as loud as they could raise their voices; whilst the women of each party, who had their goods at stake, formed into two rows on the line between the two parties of players, and danced also, in a uniform step, and all their voices joined in chants to the Great Spirit; in which they were soliciting his favor in deciding the game to their advantage; and also encouraging the players to exert every power they possessed, in the struggle that was to ensue.

A group of Choctaw posed with uplifted rackets as shown in the drawing by Catlin (1913, vol. 2, pl. 224), but the action was not explained at the time.

BULLET GAME

Many tribes of Indians have games in which an object is hidden by one group of players, the opponents guessing where it is concealed. In some tribes the object is hidden in a cane tube or wooden container, but the more familiar form of the hidden-ball game is that in which the object is hidden under a moccasin. Among the Chippewa and Sioux this is called the moccasin game. Four moccasins are laid in a row on the ground and a bullet is placed under each moccasin, one bullet being marked. The opponents guess the location of the marked bullet (Densmore, 1929, pp. 114, 115). According to Culin, "the game was borrowed by the whites and played by them under the name of 'bullet'" (Culin, 1907, p. 339). Among the Choctaw this is called the bullet game and the manner of play is similar to the Chippewa moccasin game except that folded handkerchiefs are used instead of moccasins.

Four handkerchiefs of the sort commonly used were obtained and Wesley folded them in the customary manner (pl. 21, fig. 2). The shape is not unlike that of a moccasin and they can be turned or tossed aside easily by the man making the guess. This man holds a long stick with which he turns one after another until he finds the marked bullet. It appears that only one bullet was formerly used by the Choctaw. Wesley said "the old chief dreamed about hiding a bullet under four handkerchiefs; afterward they painted the bullets with different colors." After this had been done, the game probably consisted in locating the bullet of a certain color.

Twenty-four counters or score sticks are used. The manner of keeping the score is apart from present consideration, but it is possible to make four by a correct guess, that number of counters being handed to the correct guesser by the man who hid the bullet. When a correct guess has been made the singing stops. The words of the next song were said to mean, "I will guess so well that I will make four at once." This is an assertion of success, but the words of the song show us the defeated opponent, handing four counters to the successful guesser. The songs of the bullet game are without instrumental accompaniment. There seem to have been few songs with this game, as both Wesley and Tubby said the song they recorded was the only one used during a bullet game.

No. 7. Bullet Game Song (a)

(Catalog No. 2202)

Recorded by SIDNEY WESLEY

Free translation.—Here are four counters.

Analysis.—The chief interest of this song is in the thematic treatment of the opening phrase. This is evident throughout the melody and is the more interesting as Wesley is not accustomed to singing these old songs at the present time.

No. 8. Bullet Game Song (b)

(Catalog No. 2270)

Recorded by GUS WILLIS

♩ = 144

Irregular in tonality

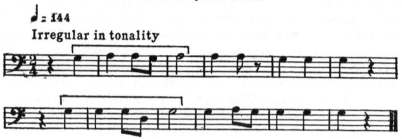

The next song was intended to confuse the opponents, so they could not guess correctly.

No. 9. Bullet Game Song (c)

(Catalog No. 2371)

Recorded by LYSANDER TUBBY

♩ = 63

Analysis.—The songs of a hidden ball game have been recorded in several tribes and are characterized by a small compass, short phrases, and a style that is somewhat exclamatory. The present melodies are examples of this style.

TICK DANCE

It has been said concerning the Choctaw that, "What they lack in ceremonialism they seem to have made up for in social feasts and dances (Cushman, 1899, p. 221)." The songs of thirteen dances were recorded in connection with the present work and no mention was made of ceremonial action with any of them. This, however, was not a subject of special inquiry.

Bushnell states,

The Choctaw living at Bayou Lacomb have one dance ceremony, which is in reality a series of seven distinct dances, performed in rotation and always in the same order. [Bushnell, 1909, pp. 20–22, pls. 21, 22.]

These dances are Man dance, Tick dance, Drunken-man dance, Duck dance, Dance Go-and-come, and Snake dance. The songs of the Tick, Drunken-man, Duck, and Snake dances are presented in the order assigned them by this authority. The songs of the three other dances were not recorded, though it is possible that further inquiry might identify them with recorded songs. At a dance attended by the writer, at Pearl River on the Choctaw reservation, the order of dances was as follows—Tick dance, Steal-partner dance, Bear dance, and Snake dance. These were followed by the Stomp dance, which was given by request. The dancing was outdoors at night, by the light of a fire at one side of the dance circle.

The leader of the singing may dance, if he is a young man, taking his place at the head of the long line of dancers. If he is an older man he "just sings," standing in the middle of the dance circle. The information on the number of singers with all the dances is not entirely clear, but it was said that the leader sings alone in the Quail and Chicken dances, that only the men sing in the Stomp dance, and that everyone sings in the Tick, Steal-partner, Snake, and War dances. The leader begins the song, followed after a short phrase by the others, the women singing an octave above the men. If striking sticks are used, the leader is the only man who provides this accompaniment. The dances with this accompaniment, as stated, are the Bear, Quail. Duck, Terrapin, Turkey, Chicken, and Pleasure dances.

Tick Dance

Men, women, and children take part in this dance and all join in the singing. Wesley said they form in a long line with the men in advance and move slowly, the step consisting in advancing the left foot, bringing the right foot to a position beside it and standing for a moment on both feet before again going forward. To this description Bushnell adds a statement that—

When they take the forward step they stamp with the right foot, as if crushing ticks on the ground, at the same time looking down, supposedly at the doomed insects.[13]

This dance has many songs, all being sung without accompaniment.

---

[13] Bushnell, 1909, pp. 20–22. A song of the Tick dance is presented in musical notation and the action of other dances is described.

No. 10. Tick Dance Song (a)

(Catalog No. 2200)

Recorded by SIDNEY WESLEY

Analysis.—The rhythm of this melody is strongly marked, this quality of the melody taking the place of an instrumental accompaniment. The interest of the rhythm centers in the slight variations of the rhythmic unit which produce a swaying effect. The first and second occurrences of the unit begin with a descending progression and the third and fourth occurrences begin with an ascending progression, which produces an effect of swaying. The song has a compass of five tones and contains only the tones of the minor triad and fourth.

No. 11. Tick Dance Song (b)

(Catalog No. 2201)

Recorded by SIDNEY WESLEY

Analysis.—This song is the first example of the period formation described on page 118. The second period is distinguished by changes of tempo and phrases containing small count-divisions. Two descending, over-lapping fourths occur frequently, these being C–G and A–E, but the principal interval in the framework of the melody is the minor third between E and G. A minor third comprises 38 of the 65 intervals.

No. 12. Tick Dance Song (c)

(Catalog No. 2210)

Recorded by SIDNEY WESLEY

Analysis.—This resembles the song next preceding in its period formation. The phrases in period A are long and contain two rythmic units. Period B contains frequent short rests and no rhythmic unit. A whole tone is the most frequent interval of progression. The pitch was gradually raised a semitone during the singing of this song, a mannerism occurring in no other performance by the Choctaw. It occurs frequently in Pueblo songs and is given extended consideration in Music of Santo Domingo Pueblo (Densmore, 1938, pp. 52–54) ; also in unpublished material on songs of Acoma, Isleta, and Cochiti Pueblos and the Seminole (mss. in Bur. Amer. Ethnol.).

No. 13. Tick Dance Song (d)

(Catalog No. 2215)

Recorded by Sidney Wesley

Analysis.—The emphatic rhythm of this song, together with the rise and fall of the melody, takes the place of an instrumental accompaniment. The song contains no change of measure length, thus maintaining a steady rhythm. Three rhythmic units occur. The second and third units differ in only one tone, but this difference was given with distinctness. The melody lies partly above and partly below the keynote, and contains only the tones of the minor triad and fourth.

Another song of this dance, recorded by Wesley but not transcribed, was difficult to translate. The interpreter first said the words meant, "My friend, this song is going away mocking me," and added that the second word was literally "people," but understood to mean "friend," also that the word translated "mocking" did not carry any unpleasant meaning, but could also be translated "imitating." There was considerable discussion and it developed that reference was being made to the phonograph which would repeat the sound of Wesley's voice. The final translation appeared to be addressed to the phonograph and was as follows, "My friend, when you go away you will sing like I sing." In another tribe a singer referred to the phonograph as a personality saying, "How did it learn the song so quick? That is a hard song."

Lysander Tubby, who recorded many songs of this dance, said that, at a dance, each song is sung three times, this series being called "once through the song," after which another song is started. Tubby is leader of the singers at Pearl River, where the writer witnessed this dance. The leader started each song and after two or three measures the men took up the melody, followed, after about the same time, by the women singers.

No. 14. Tick Dance Song (e)

(Catalog No. 2357)

Recorded by LYSANDER TUBBY

Analysis.—This song has a compass of 11 tones, which is the largest in the Choctaw songs. It is based chiefly on the major triad with an emphasis on E in the lower octave.

No. 15. Tick Dance Song (f)

(Catalog No. 2358)

Recorded by LYSANDER TUBBY

Analysis.—Only the tones of a minor third and fourth occur in this song. The general trend is a descending fourth followed by an ascending and descending minor third. This transcription contains a minus sign over one note, showing the tone was slightly below the indicated pitch in all the renditions. Other songs containing this sign are Nos. 17, 36, and 38.

No. 16. Tick Dance Song (g)

(Catalog No. 2370)

Recorded by LYSANDER TUBBY

Analysis.—This melody is based on intervals, not on the relationship of tones to a keynote. As in similar songs, the signature is used for convenience in showing the pitch of the tones, not as an indication of *key* in the musician's use of that term. Three descending fourths form the framework of the melody. In the order of occurrence there are A flat–E flat, B flat–F, and E flat–B flat.

In this and the two songs next following a second singer joined, as the dancers would join the leader in singing.

No. 17. Tick Dance Song (h)

(Catalog No. 2374)

Recorded by LYSANDER TUBBY and GUS WILLIS

Analysis.—The keynote and fifth are the most prominent tones in this melody. The tone transcribed as G sharp was clearly sung, also the augmented second which follows. Gus Willis joined with Tubby in this song to show the manner in which other singers join the leader. His voice entered on the fourth measure and continued in unison with Tubby's. Other songs in which Willis joined are Nos. 18, 19, 25, 26, 33, and 35. This "second part" is not indicated in the transcriptions (cf. p. 121).

No. 18. Tick Dance Song (i)

(Catalog No. 2375)

Recorded by LYSANDER TUBBY and GUS WILLIS

No. 19. Tick Dance Song (j)

(Catalog No. 2376)

Recorded by LYSANDER TUBBY and GUS WILLIS

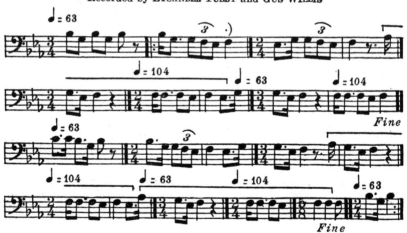

Analysis.—With the exception of one tone, each of these melodies lies within the compass of a fifth and its principal tones are those of a major triad. A majority of the intervals are descending progressions, and the performance ended on the tone above the keynote.

The next song was explained as follows: "In this song a man says he has danced so much that he has lost his wife but he don't mind it."

No. 20. Tick Dance Song (k)

(Catalog No. 2352)

Recorded by OLMAN COMBY

Analysis.—This melody as recorded by Olman Comby is more melodious and less rhythmic than the six preceding versions of the Tick dance song sung by Lysander Tubby. Comby is an Indian policeman at the agency and expressed familiarity with Choctaw customs in other localities. The tonality of this song is major but the minor third below the keynote is a prominent interval. The descent to this tone produces a minor triad with minor seventh, the tones being in descending order. In structure the song may be said to consist of two overlapping triads, the upper being major and the lower being minor. The song has a compass of an octave and lies partly above and partly below the keynote.

DRUNKEN-MAN DANCE

No information was obtained concerning this dance among the Choctaw. Several songs of a dance with the same name were recorded among the Seminole in Florida and the Seminole informant said the name did not give a correct impression. He said the dancers acted as though they were happy and exuberant—so happy that they appeared as though intoxicated, but that there was no idea of actual drunkenness in the minds of the Indians.[14] A song of this dance, in musical notation, is presented by Bushnell (1909, p. 21), who describes the dance as follows:

Two lines facing each other are formed by the dancers, who lock arms. The lines slowly approach, then move backward, and then again approach. All endeavor to keep step, and during the dance all sing.

An example of the songs is presented, following this description.

---

[14] Unpublished material, Bureau of American Ethnology.

No. 21. Drunken-man Dance Song (a)

(Catalog No. 2355)

Recorded by Robert Henry

No. 22. Drunken-man Dance Song (b)

(Catalog No. 2363)

Recorded by Lysander Tubby

No. 23. Drunken-man Dance Song (c)

(Catalog No. 2364)

Recorded by LYSANDER TUBBY

No. 24. Drunken-man Dance Song (d)

(Catalog No. 2365)

Recorded by LYSANDER TUBBY

No. 25. Drunken-man Dance Song (e)

(Catalog No. 2379)

Recorded by LYSANDER TUBBY and GUS WILLIS

No. 26. Drunken-man Dance Song (f)

(Catalog No. 2380)

Recorded by LYSANDER TUBBY and GUS WILLIS

No. 27. Drunken-man Dance Song (g)

(Catalog No. 2381)

Recorded by LYSANDER TUBBY

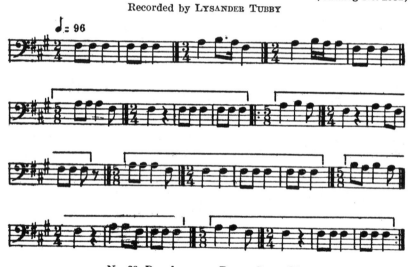

No. 28. Drunken-man Dance Song (h)

(Catalog No. 2382)

Recorded by LYSANDER TUBBY

Analysis.—The Drunken-man dance songs (Nos. 21–28) are simple and do not require detailed analysis. A majority of the melodies are based on a major or minor triad and the count divisions consist chiefly of quarter and eighth notes. A nota legato occurs in Nos. 23 and 26, and a swaying effect is given by the melody and rhythm of No. 26, a melody lying partly above and partly below the keynote. The melodic material of No. 26 consists of a tone (regarded as the keynote) with a minor third above and a whole tone below that tone. In No. 27 the only tones are a keynote with its minor third and fourth. The keynote in No. 28 is F, but the third above that tone does not occur. This song contains a more varied rhythm than other songs of this dance.

DUCK DANCE

The action of this dance appears to consist of two parts, each imitating the ducks. The dancers are in couples, two men holding hands and facing two women who also hold each other's hands. The men raise their hands and the women stoop and pass underneath, this being "like ducks going under water." The women are then face-to-face with two other men who, in turn, raise their hands and the women again "dive" underneath. It was also said that the dancers *slip* their feet back and forth, at first slowly and then faster until the motion is a "fast shuffle." The singer leads in the motion. In songs of the Duck dance and the Quail dance the tempo was gradually increased, to correspond with the motion that has been described. This change is not shown in the transcription. The songs of this dance were accompanied by the striking of sticks. Wesley made these and brought them with him when coming to record songs on the second day (cf. p. 122 and pl. 16, fig. 1).

In describing the Duck dance, Bushnell says (1909, p. 21):

Partners are required in this dance also; they form two lines, facing. The peculiar feature is that two partners pass under the arms of another couple, as shown in plate 21. The dancers endeavor to imitate the motion of a duck in walking, hence the name of the dance.

No. 29. Duck Dance Song (a)

(Catalog No. 2203)

Recorded by SIDNEY WESLEY

Fine

Analysis.—The principal interval in this song is the major third from G to B, followed by a descent to D in some measures and to E in others. Thus the tonality seems to waver between major and minor. With a single exception the rhythmic unit occurs on one series of tones, suggesting the repetition of a single motion in the dance. The opening phrase is energetic, the rhythmic unit is brisk, and the whole song is lively and interesting.

No. 30. Duck Dance Song (b)

(Catalog No. 2269)

Recorded by GUS WILLIS

Voice ♩ = 132
Striking sticks ♩ = 132
See rhythm of striking sticks below

Rhythm of striking sticks

Analysis.—Repetitions of the rhythmic unit constitute this entire melody, with the progressions alike on the second and alternate phrases. These suggest a major triad, while the first phrase and alternate phrases are based on a minor triad. The tone material is that of the fourth 5-toned scale,[15] and about two-thirds of the intervals are whole tones. The striking sticks are in the same meter as the voice, but each stroke slightly preceded the voice, as though hastening it.

SNAKE DANCE

This is last of the dances named in prescribed order by Bushnell, and was fourth in order of the dances seen by the writer. The dance is common to many tribes and has been seen, by the writer, among the Winnebago and Menominee in Wisconsin. Men and women take part in the dance, holding hands in a long line and following a leader.

---

[15] See footnote to table 6, p. 186.

At first they move in sinuous curves, then in a wide circle that gradually narrows until the dancers are in a compact mass with the leader in the middle. By a series of clever maneuvers, he then unfolds the line of dancers until they are again in a long line. The latter part of this performance differs from the description by Bushnell which represents the custom among the Choctaw at Bayou Lacomb, La.[16] The songs among the Choctaw of Mississippi are without instrumental accompaniment. Snake dance songs recorded among the Seminole were also without accompaniment.

No. 31. Snake Dance Song (a)

(Catalog No. 2204)

Recorded by SIDNEY WESLEY

---

[16] In the snake dance "the dancers form in a single line, either grasping hands or each holding on to the shoulder of the dancer immediately in front. First come the men, then the women, and lastly the boys and girls, if any are to dance. The first man in the line is naturally the leader; he moves along in a serpentine course, all following. Gradually he leads the dancers around and around until the line becomes coiled, in form resembling a snake. Soon the coil becomes so close it is impossible to move farther; thereupon the participants release their hold on one another and cease dancing. As will be seen, the song belonging to this dance is very simple, but it is repeated many, many times, being sung during the entire time consumed by the dance, said to be an hour or more" (Bushnell, 1909, pp. 21, 22, and pl. 22). A song of this dance, in musical notation, is presented by Bushnell, also illustrations showing the action of the dancers.

No. 32. Snake Dance Song (b)

(Catalog No. 2373)

Recorded by LYSANDER TUBBY

Analysis.—These two songs (Nos. 31, 32), recorded by different singers, are practically the same in the first portion but differ in the second portion which was repeated an indefinite number of times in the dancing. The first song is the more interesting and contains a change of tempo. The second song maintains the original tempo and was sung by the customary leader of the dance. The original tempo and pitch are about the same in the two songs. As in many other Choctaw songs, the framework is that of a triad with the third as the highest tone.

The following dances are not mentioned by Bushnell. The Steal-partner, Bear, and Stomp dances were witnessed by the writer.

STEAL-PARTNER DANCE

Men and women took part in this dance, and Wesley said "they dance a long time with the first partner and then change to the second." No further description was obtained. The songs are without instrumental accompaniment.

No. 33. Steal-partner Dance Song (a)

(Catalog No. 2377)

Recorded by LYSANDER TUBBY and GUS WILLIS

Translation.—I am stealing from you.   You are not trying to get it back.

Analysis.—A change of tonality from major to minor without a change of keynote occurs in this song and is indicated in the transcription. The descending fourth is prominent throughout the melody.

No. 34. Steal-partner Dance Song (b)

(Catalog No. 2359)

Recorded by LYSANDER TUBBY

No. 35. Steal-partner Dance Song (c)

(Catalog No. 2378)

Recorded by Lysander Tubby and Gus Willis

No. 36. Steal-partner Dance Song (d)

(Catalog No. 2360)

Recorded by Lysander Tubby

No. 37. Steal-partner Dance Song (e)

(Catalog No. 2361)

Recorded by Lysander Tubby

Fine

No. 38. Steal-partner Dance Song (f)

(Catalog No. 2362)

Recorded by LYSANDER TUBBY

Analysis.—The first song of this group (Nos. 34–38) begins with a minor third and is clearly minor in tonality, but the others begin with a major third, followed by a descent of a minor third completing a minor triad. Nos. 35, 36, and 37 were recorded on the same day, with several renditions of each, and No. 38 was recorded a few days later. On comparing the transcriptions, we note such a resemblance in general form that they might, possibly, be regarded as variants of a single melody. The singer, however, was a man of unusual ability and experience and the Steal-partner dance is a popular dance, employing many songs. Under these circumstances it is possible that close resemblances might occur in the melodies, which he recorded without hesitation. The most elaborate of these songs is No. 38, which contains three rhythmic units, numerous measures in 5-8 time, and several occurrences of nota legato. In Nos. 33 and 35 Gus Willis joined the singer after the first phrase, the voices continuing in unison (cf. p. 121).

No. 39. Steal-partner Dance Song (g)

(Catalog No. 2205)

Recorded by SIDNEY WESLEY

Analysis.—The two parts of this song were separated by a pause in the recording. The first part is based on the fourth 5-toned scale and if the second part were a tone higher, it would correspond to the upper portion of that series. It is transcribed as sung, and we note that the second part is on a minor third, suggesting the change from major to minor tonality that was noted in earlier songs of this dance. The rhythmic units in the two parts are the same length but differ in count divisions.

BEAR DANCE

This was said to be a "hard jumping dance." It could be held at any time and the dancers were men and women, moving in couples around the circle and preceded by a leader. The songs were accompanied by the striking sticks, carried by the leader who also led the singing and the "yells," which were frequently given between renditions of the songs. Wesley, who recorded the next song, said "when the song goes up higher the dancers step harder and all *holler*." He probably referred to the fourth and sixth long phrases in which the tone D, as recorded, was shouted rather than sung. The pitch of this tone can be indicated only approximately in notation.

No. 40. Bear Dance Song (a)

(Catalog No. 2192)

Recorded by SIDNEY WESLEY

Voice ♩= 88
Striking sticks ♩= 88
Rhythm of striking sticks similar to No. 30

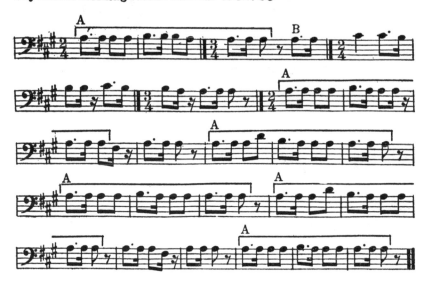

Analysis.—An interesting change of rhythm occurs in this melody. The divisions of the five counts beginning with the last count in the third measure are the same as in the two preceding measures, but a change of accent produces a different rhythm. A whole tone comprises one-half the progressions, next in frequency being a minor third. This melody contains the period formation, but the form is not so clear as in the song next following.

No. 41. Bear Dance Song (b)

(Catalog No. 2264)

Recorded by ROBERT HENRY

♩= 84

Analysis.—A minor triad forms the framework of period A in this melody. Period B opens with an ascent to the seventh, the melody then descending on the tones of a minor triad and minor seventh, a sequence of tones characterizing primitive music. Period B is in double time in its first occurrence and in triple time in its second occurrence. The melody tones are those of the second 5-toned scale.

The man who recorded the next two songs was formerly a leader in the Bear dance. He said that, in the dance, they sang the first of these songs twice, then changed the step, and sang the second song twice, and then repeated the first song.

No. 42. Bear Dance Song (c)

(Catalog No. 2267)

Recorded by GUS WILLIS

Voice ♩ = 88
Striking sticks ♩ = 88
Rhythm of striking sticks similar to No. 30

No. 43. Bear Dance Song (d)

(Catalog No. 2268)

Recorded by GUS WILLIS

Voice ♩= 88
Striking sticks ♩= 88
Rhythm of striking sticks similar to No. 30

Analysis.—The short rhythmic unit in the first of these songs is extended in the second. A major triad forms the framework of the first song and the middle phrase of the second, followed by a distinct change of rhythm and a descent to E, introducing a minor triad and minor seventh with the tones in descending order. The "shouts" with the two songs were different, those which preceded and followed the first song being shown as nearly as possible in the transcription. The second song is in the same tempo as the first. The "shouts" were different and are not indicated. The melody tones of both songs are those of the fourth 5-toned scale and the number of progressions is the same in both songs, comprising 12 descending and 9 ascending intervals. Variety is given to the rhythm of the striking sticks by a change to 2 eighth-note beats on the last count of each triple measure.

STOMP DANCE

This is not one of the dances that are given in prescribed order. On the occasion of the writer's visit, the Stomp dance was given by request, following the other dances. Men and women stood in a circle, facing the center. They were not in couples but in any desired order, and all joined in the songs. The leader of the singing was an old man, who stood in the middle of the circle. As stated, the leader of the singing need not take part in the dancing, though a young man usually leads the line of dancers and sings. The motion of the dance consisted in jumping with both feet at once, the circle of dancers moving in a contraclockwise direction. No instrumental accompaniment was used with these songs.

A general characteristic of the 12 Stomp dance songs under analysis is their rhythmic structure. Five of these songs contain three rhythmic units, 3 have 2 rhythmic units, 3 have 1 rhythmic unit, and 1 song contains no unit in its first rendition and 2 rhythmic units in its repetition by the same singer. A period formation occurs in 5 of these songs (Nos. 45, 46, 48, 49, and 51). The first 8 songs were recorded by Sidney Wesley and their complicated rhythms were sung with remarkable clearness. The remaining four songs were recorded each by a different singer and are less elaborate than the songs recorded by Wesley. A variation or change in the Stomp dance is the Backward-and-forward dance (cf. No. 56, p. 171).

No. 44. Stomp Dance Song (a)

(Catalog No. 2194)

Recorded by SIDNEY WESLEY

Analysis.—This melody contains only the tones B flat and D flat except the occurrence of E flat in three measures. The three rhythmic units are in triple time and change to double time, but the count divisions in each are different. Ascending and descending intervals are equal in number, each consisting of 12 minor thirds and 3 fourths.

No. 45. Stomp Dance Song (b)

(Catalog No. 2195)

Recorded by Sidney Wesley

Analysis.—A period formation characterizes this song, the second period being short and higher in pitch than the remainder of the melody. The most prominent interval is the whole tone between F sharp and G sharp. Except for one ascending fourth, the intervals consist of whole tones and minor thirds.

No. 46. Stomp Dance Song (c)

(Catalog No. 2196)

Recorded by SIDNEY WESLEY

Analysis.—In period formation this resembles the song next preceding. The highest tone occurs in the second period, as in a majority of songs with this form. In approaching this high tone, the singer overreached the interval and sang D sharp instead of D. The next note was B, after which he gradually lowered the pitch level until the final tone of the measure was A, as transcribed. This change in pitch level was clearly unintentional and is not shown in the transcription. The second period resembles the third rhythmic unit, but the change in the rhythm of the first count gives emphasis to the phrase.

No. 47. Stomp Dance Song (d)

(Catalog No. 2197)

Recorded by SIDNEY WESLEY

Translation.—Tobacco I will smoke, bring me fire (a light?).   I am going to dance.

Analysis.—The keynote is the highest tone in this song and does not occur in the lower octave. The song is major in tonality, but about one-fourth of the intervals are minor thirds. The intervals of a major third and major sixth do not occur, and the fourth is a prominent interval. Ascending and descending progressions are about equal in number. The third measure is an interesting phrase and occurs at the close of each rhythmic unit.

No. 48. Stomp Dance Song (e)

(Catalog No. 2198)

Recorded by SIDNEY WESLEY

Analysis.—An alternation of ascending and descending phrases characterizes this melody and produces a swaying effect. Attention is directed to the sixth and seventh measures which resemble the second rhythmic unit but are in double instead of triple time. The length of the periods is similar to that in the two preceding songs of this group.

No. 49. Stomp Dance Song (f)

(Catalog No. 2199)

Recorded by SIDNEY WESLEY

Analysis.—This lively song contains only the tones of a major triad and second. The characteristic interval is a fourth, which comprises almost half the progressions. This occurs generally as a descending followed by an ascending interval.

No. 50. Stomp Dance Song (g)

(Catalog No. 2211)

Recorded by SIDNEY WESLEY

Analysis.—Three rhythmic units occur in this song, the second measure being the same in all. There is no change of measure lengths, which is unusual in Indian songs. The tones are those of the fourth 5-toned scale and the melody is framed chiefly on the descending fourths C–G, and B flat–F, the former being a broken and the latter a direct progression. The descending intervals are more than double the ascending intervals in number.

No. 51. Stomp Dance Song (h)

(Catalog No. 2216)

Recorded by SIDNEY WESLEY

First rendition

Second rendition

Analysis.—Two renditions of this song, by the same singer, are presented for comparison. It will be noted that the principal phrase is the same in each. This occurs first in the third measure of the first rendition and appears throughout both performances. The first rendition is characterized by a period formation that does not appear in the second. The rhythmic unit of this performance is interrupted by the vigorous phrase designated as period B. The melody tones of both renditions are those of the fourth 5-toned scale and the song progresses chiefly by whole tones and minor thirds.

No. 52. Stomp Dance Song (i)

(Catalog No. 2271)

Recorded by Gus Willis

First rendition

Second rendition

Analysis.—Two renditions of this song were recorded and both are presented, the second followed by the first after a short pause. Slight differences occur and will be readily noted. The tones, the tempo, and the pitch of the two are the same, also the use of two rhythmic units. The first rendition contains an introductory phrase which is indicated as a rhythmic unit. This does not occur in the repetition of the song.

No. 53. Stomp Dance Song (j)

(Catalog No. 2372)

Recorded by LYSANDER TUBBY

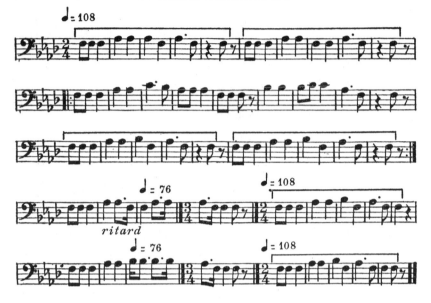

No. 54. Stomp Dance Song (k)

(Catalog No. 2354)

Recorded by ROBERT HENRY

No. 55. Stomp Dance Song (1)

(Catalog No. 2353)

Recorded by OLMAN COMBY

Analysis.—These songs (Nos. 53–55) are minor in tonality. The keynote is the lowest tone in each, and the principal progression is between this tone and its third. Nos. 54 and 55 contain the tones of the complete triad. The rhythm of these songs is simple, and the rhythmic units in Nos. 54 and 55 contain only one measure. When transcribing No. 53, a sharp sound was heard on the record. This was identified as the barking of Tubby's dog, which was allowed in the room while he recorded his songs.

An additional Stomp dance song recorded by Willis was not transcribed. This melody consists entirely of ascending and descending fourths, repeated rhythmically and forming a brief melodic phrase.

According to Wesley, the Backward-and-forward dance was a "variation or change in the Stomp dance."

No. 56. Backward-and-forward Dance Song

(Catalog No. 2206)

Recorded by SIDNEY WESLEY

Analysis.—Three periods comprise this melody, each having its own rhythmic unit. The second period begins on a higher tone, but the remainder of the melody contains only the tones A and B.

TERRAPIN, QUAIL, TURKEY, CHICKEN, AND PLEASURE DANCES

The five dances next following may be held at any time. The dancers are in couples, a man and a woman dancing together. They move four times around the circle, moving in a contraclockwise direction, singing one song. After circling four times, they begin another song. The leader of the singing is usually the leader of the dancers, taking his place at the head of the line. However, if he is an old man he is excused from leading the dancers and stands within the circle, singing and beating the striking sticks together to mark the time. The origin of these dances was not ascertained.

No. 57. Terrapin Dance Song (a)

(Catalog No. 2207)

Recorded by SIDNEY WESLEY

Analysis.—This melody consists of four repetitions of the rhythmic unit. In three of its occurrences it is preceded by an unaccented tone and in the first by an accented half note. The tone material is that of the fourth 5-toned scale and about half the progressions are whole tones. An increase in tempo, customary in the dance, is shown in the transcription.

No. 58. Terrapin Dance Song (b)

(Catalog No. 2356)

Recorded by ROBERT HENRY

Voice ♩ = 72
Striking sticks ♩ = 72
See rhythm of striking sticks below

Rhythm of striking sticks

Analysis.—The descent of an octave in the first and second measures of this song is interesting and unusual. A long descent occurs four times in the song, each descent being in two measures. The rhythmic unit is modified in the closing measures of the melody.

A characteristic of the Quail and Duck dances (Nos. 29, 30) is a gradual increase in time, possibly associated with the motion of the birds. The leader sang alone in this dance, and the songs were accompanied by the striking sticks.

No. 59. Quail Dance Song

(Catalog No. 2265)

Recorded by SIDNEY HENRY

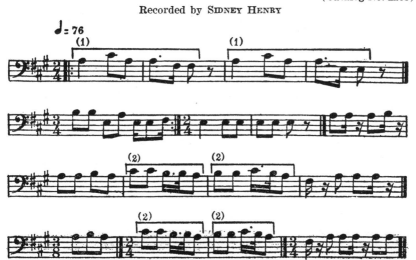

Analysis.—The principal interval in this song is a major third (A–C sharp), which is followed in the second measure by a descent to F sharp, forming a minor triad, and in the fourth measure by a descent to E, completing a major triad. This form continues throughout the song and has been noted in numerous other Choctaw songs. Two rhythmic units occur, and the melody progresses by 18 ascending and 19 descending intervals. The tempo increased from ♩=76 to ♩=92 in the repetitions of the song.

The step of the Turkey dance consists of a hop with both feet together, first one foot and then the other being placed forward. The song of this dance has words, but their meaning is not known at the present time. It is undoubtedly an old song.

No. 60. Turkey Dance Song

(Catalog No. 2209)

Recorded by Sidney Wesley

Voice ♩ = 72
Striking sticks ♩ = 72
See rhythm of striking sticks below

Rhythm of striking sticks

Analysis.—This melody is an interesting example of period formation, the second period being short, higher in pitch than the first and different in rhythm. A recurrence of the first period closes the song. Two rhythmic units occur, neither being in the second period. The first unit is based on a minor third and the second on the interval of a fourth, these units occurring chiefly in descending progression. Fourths and whole tones are equal in number, which is unusual in Indian songs. A swaying motion, with ascending and descending intervals in rapid succession, characterizes this and has been noted in other Choctaw dance songs.

The Chicken dance is usually the last dance at a gathering, and the dancers do not join in the songs, the leader singing alone.

No. 61. Chicken Dance Song

(Catalog No. 2193)

Recorded by SIDNEY WESLEY

Voice ♩ = 63
Striking sticks ♩ = 63
Rhythm of striking sticks similar to No. 60
Irregular in tonality

Analysis.—This was the first song recorded by Sidney Wesley. After he had recorded a second song, he expressed dissatisfaction with his first performance, saying he had not recorded the entire song and asking that another record be made. This was done, and the transcription is from his second recording of the song. On comparing the two performances, it was found that the first did not contain the third period. This, together with the intricate rhythm of the song, is an evidence of musical ability on the part of the singer. An entire change of rhythm occurs in the second period which is made emphatic by an accent on a sixteenth note. Four rhythmic units are shown in the transcription. The fourth unit begins with an unaccented tone, the next measure comprising the latter portion of the third rhythmic unit. About half the intervals are whole tones, and the fourths and major thirds are equal in number.

In the Pleasure dance the men are in one row and the women in another row, facing them. They move their hands up and down, as though shaking corn in a basket, all moving their hands together. The word yoha means "shift," and the men said, "yoha," the women responding "ha." The syllables transcribed with the song are probably adaptations of these words.

No. 62. Pleasure Dance Song

(Catalog No. 2214)

Recorded by SIDNEY WESLEY

Voice ♩= 69
Striking sticks ♩= 69
Rhythm of striking sticks similar to No. 30

Analysis.—The opening phrases of this song contain two descending fourths followed by two ascending fourths. In the fourth and fifth measures are found three consecutive ascending fourths with a slight prolonging of the highest tone. The tempo of the striking sticks was not maintained steadily, sometimes being slightly faster than the tempo of the voice.

HUNTING SONG

The blowgun was formerly the weapon used by the Choctaw in hunting small animals and birds. Robert Henry demonstrated the use of this weapon when the writer visited his home. He knelt on one knee, threw back his head, held the blowgun high in the air, and shot the dart a long distance.[17] A blowgun and two darts from the Choctaw of Louisiana, is in the possession of the United States National Museum. The darts are wrapped with ravelled cloth at the base and are 18 inches in length. The blowgun shows "long use and wear," and is 87½ inches long.

---

[17] "The primitive blowgun was used until recently in hunting squirrels, rabbits, and various birds. Only one specimen was found at Bayou Lacomb; this was said to have been made some 10 years ago. . . . The blowgun . . . is about 7 feet in length; it is made of a single piece of cane . . . formed into a tube by perforation of the joints, which was given a smooth bore of uniform diameter throughout. The darts . . . are made of either small, slender canes or pieces of hard yellow pine, sharpened at one end; they are from 15 to 18

A very old hunting song was recorded by both Lysander Tubby and Robert Henry. The words of the two renditions were the same except that Henry omitted the second line. His rendition was transcribed and studied, but lacks the clearness of Tubby's, which is presented. Henry's was a simpler version of the melody, and it will be recalled that his version of the song for success in the ball game was simpler than that of Willis (cf. No. 6).

No. 63. Hunting Song

(Catalog No. 2272)

Recorded by LYSANDER TUBBY

Translation

Go and grind some corn, we will go camping,
Go and sew, we will go camping,
I passed on and you were sitting there crying,
You were lazy and your hoe is rusty.

inches in length. The lower end is wrapped for a distance of 4 or 5 inches with a narrow band of cloth having a frayed edge, or a piece of soft tanned skin is used. The effect of this band is to expand and fill the bore of the gun, a result that could not possibly be secured by the use of feathers, as in the case of ordinary arrows" (Bushnell, 1909, p. 18).

Analysis.—The entire performance of this song was transcribed and occupied 2 minutes. In tonality the song is minor, the tones being those of the second 5-toned scale. A slight change in tempo occurred, the change being gradual, and the original tempo resumed after a few measures. This change took place in each rendition. Phrases in the latter portion of the song were sometimes sung in a slightly faster tempo, but the change was not clear enough to be indicated in the transcription. Probably these changes in tempo were connected with the words of the song.

SONGS CONNECTED WITH PASTIMES

A pastime entitled "Rabbit in the Garden" was accompanied by a song of the same name. In describing the occasion for singing this song, Wesley said the women held hands forming a circle. This represented a garden and the women were the fence around it. In the middle of the circle were a boy and girl, representing rabbits, who tried to get out, but were prevented by the women. The words are evidently sung by rote as the terms "ladies' chain" and "putting in the garden" are used without meaning and the word "chain" was pronounced "chan." The word was identified by the interpreter.

This is evidently the song of an old folk-play, learned by the Indians from white settlers and handed down for several generations. A song, entitled "Rabbit in the Hollow," with a description of the action, is found in a book of folk games and dances (Hofer, 1907, p. 23). The words are in German and are translated "rabbit in the hollow sits and sleeps." The meter of these words is exactly the same as the meter of "rabbit in the garden, can't come out" except that, in one instance, two eighth notes take the place of one quarter note. There is a resemblance in the meter of the remainder of the song.

An inquiry was made of Dr. John R. Swanton as to whether the Choctaw were ever in contact with German settlers, and he replied as follows:

Colonies of Germans were planted here and there in various parts of the South, Germany being then a people but not a nation, but I recall none in or near the Choctaw country. There was one such colony, Les Allemands, on the lower Mississippi, and a colony of Salzburgers from the Palatinate about Ebenezer Creek on Savannah River. . . . It occurs to me that there may be some connection between this song and the story of how Brer Rabbit deceived the little girl and got out of the garden. This is widely spread in the South and was used by Joel Chandler Harris.

No. 64. "Rabbit in the Garden"

(Catalog No. 2212)

Recorded by SIDNEY WESLEY

Words as recorded by the singer.—O some ladies' chain, Rabbit putting in the garden, can't come out. I bet you five dollars can't come out.

Analysis.—This melody is short and its repetitions are transcribed because of the interest in the words. The structure is clear and comprises five phrases with practically the same rhythm. There is a peculiar quality in the rhythm that would make possible the continuance of the song for a long time. The tones are those of the fourth 5-toned scale, the entire melody lying above the keynote.

A familiar scene of the hunt is dramatized in the second pastime. Only two players take part, one representing a dog and the other a raccoon. The dog chases the raccoon, which runs among the spectators, followed by the dog until it escapes. Meaningless syllables interspersed with a few words were sung with the melody, as shown in the transcription, and the words "Look out, dog, coon's gone" were spoken after the rendition of the song. These words were followed by a repetition of the song.

No. 65. A Dog Chases a Raccoon

(Catalog No. 2213)

Recorded by SIDNEY WESLEY

Analysis.—The structure of this melody is freely melodic. The song is based on consecutive descending fourths, these being C–G and B flat–F. A minor third occurs in the fourth measure and a minor triad in the measure before the spoken words. These progressions suggest G as the keynote of the song. A slow rhythmic unit and a steady rhythm characterize the song which contains no suggestion of a chase. Instead it seems to reflect the mood of an observer, as indicated by the words. The song contains 10 ascending and 9 descending intervals.

COMPARISON BETWEEN THE ANALYSES OF CHOCTAW SONGS AND
THE ANALYSES OF SONGS RECORDED IN CERTAIN OTHER TRIBES [18]

In previous books of this series, the songs of each tribe have
been compared with the total number of songs recorded and analyzed
in other tribes. This method is discontinued, and the present comparison is based on observation of the preceding work, attention
being directed to resemblances or differences that are important to
an understanding of Indian music. The purpose of these and previous comparisons is to determine the characteristics that are general and those that are peculiar to tribes and regions. When the
latter are determined, it is often possible to trace the peculiarities
to influences in or near the region. Certain bases of analysis
have been discontinued when the results were practically the same
in all the tribes under analysis, others have been discontinued for
other reasons. Only 12 tables of analysis are here presented, although 22 tables were used in Teton Sioux Music, published in 1918.
These are believed to include the most important melodic and rhythmic characteristics of the songs.

Table 1. Tonality.—The Choctaw songs contain 51 percent with
major tonality, this being approximately the average in all the songs
under analysis. The Menominee songs contained 66 percent and the
Sioux contained only 39 percent that were major in tonality, while
the cumulative analysis of 1,553 songs [19] contained 53 percent with
this tonality.

Table 2. First note of song; its relation to keynote.—Tribes differ
widely in this respect. The Choctaw group contains 47 percent beginning on the keynote, while the cumulative series contains only 13
percent with this beginning. In the Menominee songs only 5 percent begin on the keynote while 30 percent begin on the fifth above
the keynote.

Table 3. Last note of song; its relation to keynote.—A feeling for
the keynote is evident in this as in the preceding table, 59 percent
of the Choctaw songs ending on the keynote. There is an interesting uniformity in this ending, the Sioux, Papago, Menominee, and
Yuman and Yaqui groups each having 54 percent ending on the
keynote. Tribes that differ widely are the Pawnee, with 72 percent,
and the Mandan and Hidatsa, with 37 percent, ending on the keynote.

---

[18] Chippewa, Sioux, Mandan, Hidatsa, Northern Ute, Pawnee, Papago, Yuman, Yaqui,
Menominee, Nootka, and Quileute, and several Pueblo groups, these being analyzed in tables.
The songs of the Cheyenne, Arapaho, Alabama, Tule of Panama, Winnebago Indians of
Santo Domingo, N. Mex., and Indians of British Columbia were not analyzed in tables.

[19] Cf. Densmore, 1939, pp. 35–41. Songs are classified according to the tribe recording
them. Songs of another tribe are occasionally recorded, this being mentioned in the text,
but not considered in the tabulated analyses.

Table 4. Last note of song; its relation to compass of song.—The final note is the lowest in 47 percent of the Choctaw songs. In the cumulative group 68 percent, and in the Chippewa songs 88 percent end on the lowest tone of the compass. In songs having the final tone immediately preceded by a lower tone the most frequent approach is by means of an ascending minor third, 12 percent of the Choctaw and 5 percent in the cumulative group having this approach to the final tone.

Table 5. Number of tones comprised in compass of song.—The Choctaw songs are characterized by a small compass, only 19 percent having a compass of 8 or more tones. About 68 percent of the songs in the cumulative analysis have this compass. The Nootka and Quileute have only about 22 percent while the Pawnee have 72 percent and the Sioux songs have 94 percent with a compass of 8 or more tones. The Ute, Chippewa, and Mandan and Hidatsa, have respectively 89, 88, and 87 percent, and the Papago, Menominee, Yuman, and Yaqui a slightly smaller percentage of songs with this compass.

Table 6. Tone material.—This is an interesting test of Indian songs but far from conclusive. It is necessary to use the terminology of a system that is familiar to us but foreign to the Indians. Measured by this standard, we note that 29 percent of the Choctaw songs are on the "major and minor pentatonic scales" [20] and 21 percent lack only one tone of being based on these scales. Only four of the 65 Choctaw songs contain all the tones of the diatonic octave. In the cumulative analyses, 28 percent are on the second and fourth 5-toned scales.

Table 7. First progression, downward and upward.—In the Choctaw songs 57 percent begin with a downward progression. The total number of intervals in the cumulative series of 1,553 songs shows the downward trend of Indian melodies, 60 percent of the progressions being downward, yet the percentage of songs beginning with a downward progression, in this cumulative series, is only 41 percent. In the Nootka and Quileute songs only 41 percent begin with a downward progression, while 70 percent of the Chippewa and 71 percent of the Pawnee songs have this opening interval. Fifty-one percent of the Mandan and Hidatsa songs being with a descending interval, the percentages in the Papago, Yuman and Yaqui, Menominee, and Sioux being, respectively 61, 62, 63, and 69 percent.

Table 8. Part of measure on which song begins.—A direct attack is shown by the fact that 88 percent of the Choctaw songs begin on the accented count of the measure. Only 55 percent in the cumulative group have this beginning. In the various tribes the average is about

---

[20] See footnote p. 186, after table 6.

60 percent, though the Yuman and Yaqui have only 49 percent of the songs beginning on an accented tone.

Table 9. Rhythm (meter) of first measure.—Double time is preferred by the Choctaw for the beginning of their songs, 83 percent having the first measure in 2–4 time. This would be expected, as a majority of recorded Choctaw songs are dance melodies. In other tribes the songs are more varied, an attempt being made to have about the same proportion of each class of songs in a tribe. The percentages of songs beginning in 2–4 time are remarkably uniform. This percentage is 50 in the Chippewa, 54 in the Sioux and Papago, 55 and 57 in the Mandan, Hidatsa, Yuman, and Yaqui, 62 in the Pawnee, 64 in the Ute and Menominee, and 66 in the Nootka and Quileute. The percentage in the cumulative series is 60 percent.

Table 10. Change of time (measure lengths).—In the Choctaw songs 62 percent contain a change of time. This is the smallest percentage in the songs under analysis and we note again that a majority of the recorded Choctaw songs are connected with dances. Next are the Pawnee, and Yuman and Yaqui, 74 percent of the songs in each of these groups containing a change of time. The Sioux and Papago groups contain the highest percentages of songs with a change of time, these being respectively 92 and 91 percent. This shows a change of measure lengths, as indicated by accented tones, to be a prevailing characteristic of Indian songs.

Table 11. Rhythmic unit of song.—The rhythmic character of the recorded Choctaw songs is indicated by the presence of one or more rhythmic units in 88 percent of the songs. The next percentage is in the Menominee group with 87 percent having a rhythmic unit. The least rhythmic songs are found among the Nootka and Quileute, only 55 percent of these songs containing a rhythmic unit. The Pawnee group contains 84 percent and certain other groups contain 68, 70, and 76 percent of songs with rhythmic units. A large majority of these songs contain only one rhythmic unit, but others have two, three, four, or five rhythmic units.

Table 12. Rhythm (meter) of striking sticks used as an accompaniment to songs.—A limited number of Choctaw songs were recorded with the accompaniment of striking sticks, four rhythms being noted. The accompaniment was continuous, not interspersed with rests as in the Yuman and Yaqui songs (cf. Densmore, 1932, p. 208). In a compilation of 366 Chippewa and Sioux songs, 40 percent contained a drumbeat in unaccented eighth notes and 34 percent contained a drumbeat in quarter-note values, each beat preceded by an unaccented beat corresponding approximately to the third count of a triplet (cf. Densmore, 1918, p. 36). The latter occurs with 6 percent of the Choctaw songs.

Intervals of progression in Indian songs.—In tribes analyzed prior to and including the Yuman and Yaqui, a tabulation was made of the intervals in ascending and descending progression. The intervals in 36 Choctaw songs were tabulated as a test of that tribe. The total number of intervals in these songs is 1,474, of which 855 (59 percent) are descending and 619 (41 percent) are ascending progressions. This shows that the general trend of the Choctaw melodies is downward, as in other Indian songs. The largest group of intervals consists of 612 whole tones and 430 minor thirds, showing the general melodic structure to be similar to that of the other tribes under analysis.

MELODIC AND RHYTHMIC ANALYSIS OF SONGS BY SERIAL NUMBERS

MELODIC ANALYSIS

TABLE 1.—*Tonality*

Classification of song	Serial number of song	Number	Percent
Major tonality [1]	2, 3, 5, 6, 7, 11, 14, 17, 18, 19, 20, 22, 25, 30, 31, 32, 33, 39, 40, 42, 43, 46, 47, 49, 56, 57, 58, 59, 60, 64, 65.	31	48
Minor tonality [2]	9, 10, 12, 13, 15, 21, 23, 24, 26, 27, 29, 34, 35, 36, 37, 38, 41, 45, 48, 50, 51, 52, 53, 54, 55, 62, 63.	28	43
Third lacking	1, 4, 16, 28	4	6
Irregular in tonality [3]	8, 61	2	2
Total		65	

[1] Songs are thus classified if the third is a major third and the sixth, if present, is a major sixth above the keynote.
[2] Songs are thus classified if the third is a minor third and the sixth, if present, is a minor sixth above the keynote.
[3] Songs are thus classified if the tones do not have an apparent keynote. In such songs the tones appear to be arranged with reference to intervals rather than with reference to a keynote, many being based on the interval of a fourth.

TABLE 2.—*First note of song; its relation to keynote*

Classification of song	Serial number of song	Number	Percent
Beginning on the—			
Sixth	2	1	2
Fifth	12, 18, 19, 21, 29, 35, 37, 38, 39	9	14
Fourth	3, 5, 14, 15, 50, 62	6	10
Third	9, 13, 20, 34, 36, 41, 42, 51, 52, 54, 55, 57, 58, 64	14	22
Second	30, 56	2	2
Keynote	1, 4, 6, 7, 10, 11, 16, 17, 22, 23, 24, 25, 26, 27, 28, 31, 32, 33, 40, 43, 44, 45, 46, 47, 48, 49, 53, 59, 60, 63, 65.	31	47
Irregular in tonality	8, 61	2	2
Total		65	

TABLE 3.—*Last note of song; its relation to keynote*

Classification of song	Serial number of song	Number	Percent
Ending on the—			
Fifth	1, 2, 4, 7, 16, 17, 20, 28, 30, 32, 47, 60, 65	13	20
Third	9, 11, 21, 35, 38, 39, 41, 50, 57, 58	10	15
Keynote	3, 5, 6, 10, 12, 13, 14, 15, 22, 23, 24, 25, 26, 27, 29, 31, 33, 34, 36, 37, 40, 42, 43, 44, 45, 46, 48, 49, 51, 52, 53, 54, 55, 56, 59, 62, 63, 64.	38	59
Indeterminate ending	18, 19	2	2
Irregular in tonality	8, 61	2	2
Total		65	-------

TABLE 4.—*Last note of song; its relation to compass of song*

Classification of song	Serial number of song	Number	Percent
Songs in which final tone is—			
Lowest tone in song	1, 4, 5, 6, 7, 10, 11, 15, 17, 19, 20, 22, 24, 25, 27, 28, 30, 32, 36, 37, 38, 42, 44, 52, 53, 54, 56, 57, 58, 64.	30	47
Immediately preceded by [1]—			
Fourth below	13, 16, 34, 46, 47, 49, 61, 62	8	12
Minor third below	3, 21, 35, 39, 40, 41, 50, 59	8	12
Whole tone below	18, 26, 45, 48, 51, 55	6	9
Songs containing lower tones than final tone.	2, 8, 9, 12, 14, 23, 29, 31, 33, 43, 60, 63, 65	13	20
Total		65	-------

[1] This shows the approach to the final tone.   Many songs in this group contain other tones lower than the final tone.

TABLE 5.—*Number of tones comprised in compass of song*

Compass of song	Serial number of song	Number	Percent
Eleven tones	14	1	2
Ten tones	60	1	2
Eight tones	12, 13, 16, 20, 28, 32, 33, 57, 58, 63	10	15
Seven tones	3, 23, 25, 35, 38, 41, 43, 46, 47, 48, 56, 62	12	18
Six tones	2, 5, 7, 11, 17, 18, 19, 29, 30, 31, 34, 39, 40, 49, 50, 51, 53, 55, 59, 64, 65.	21	32
Five tones	1, 4, 8, 9, 10, 21, 22, 24, 26, 35, 36, 37, 45, 52, 54	15	23
Four tones	15, 27, 42, 44	4	6
Three tones	6	1	2
Total		65	-------

TABLE 6.—*Tone material*

Tonality of song	Serial number of song	Number	Percent
Second 5-toned scale [1]	7, 17, 20, 30, 39, 43, 51, 63	8	12
Fourth 5-toned scale	23, 24, 29, 41, 50, 53, 55, 57, 59, 60, 64	11	17
Major triad and one other tone	18, 22, 31, 49	4	6
Minor triad and one other tone	9, 10, 13, 15, 34, 36, 37, 38, 52, 54	10	15
Octave complete	32, 33, 46, 48	4	6
Other combinations of tones	1, 2, 3, 4, 5, 6, 8, 11, 12, 14, 16, 19, 21, 25, 26, 27, 28, 35, 40, 42, 44, 45, 47, 56, 58, 61, 62, 65.	28	44
Total		65	-------

[1] The 5-toned scales considered in these analyses are two of the 5-toned scales according to Helmholtz, described by him as follows:

"*To the Second Scale*, without Second or Sixth, belong most Scotch airs which have a minor character . . . .

"*To the Fourth Scale*, without Fourth or Seventh, belong most Scotch airs which have the character of a major mode" (Helmholtz, 1885, pp. 260, 261).

TABLE 7.—*First progressions; downward and upward*

Progression	Serial number of song	Number	Percent
Downward	1, 2, 3, 4, 5, 11, 12, 14, 15, 16, 18, 19, 21, 23, 29, 30, 33, 34, 35, 36, 37, 38, 42, 46, 47, 49, 50, 51, 52, 54, 55, 56, 57, 58, 62, 63, 65.	37	57
Upward	6, 7, 8, 9, 10, 13, 17, 20, 22, 24, 25, 26, 27, 28, 31, 32, 39, 40, 41, 43, 44, 45, 48, 53, 59, 60, 61, 64.	28	43
Total		65	-------

RHYTHMIC ANALYSIS

TABLE 8.—*Part of measure on which song begins*

Beginning of song	Serial number of song	Number	Percent
On unaccented part of measure	3, 4, 5, 8, 20, 39, 52, 61	8	12
On accented part of measure	1, 2, 6, 7, 9, 10, 11, 12, 13, 14, 15, 16, 17, 18, 19, 21, 22, 23, 24, 25, 26, 27, 28, 29, 30, 31, 32, 33, 34, 35, 36, 37, 38, 40, 41, 42, 43, 44, 45, 46, 47, 48, 49, 50, 51, 53, 54, 55, 56, 57, 58, 59, 60, 62, 63, 64, 65.	57	88
Total		65	-------

TABLE 9.—*Rhythm (meter) of first measure*

Rhythm first measure	Serial number of song	Number	Percent
2–4 time	1, 3, 4, 5, 6, 7, 8, 9, 10, 11, 12, 13, 15, 16, 17, 18, 20, 21, 22, 23, 24, 25, 26, 27, 28, 29, 30, 31, 32, 33, 34, 37, 39, 40, 41, 42, 43, 44, 45, 50, 51, 52, 53, 54, 55, 56, 57, 58, 59, 60, 62, 63, 64, 65.	54	83
3–4 time	2, 14, 19, 35, 36, 46, 47, 48, 49, 61	10	15
5–8 time	38	1	2
Total		65	-------

TABLE 10.—*Change of time (measure lengths)*

Songs	Serial number of song	Number	Percent
Containing no change of time	3, 5, 6, 8, 9, 10, 13, 14, 15, 17, 22, 23, 24, 25, 26, 28, 30, 34, 37, 42, 50, 56, 59, 60, 62.	25	38
Containing a change of time	1, 2, 4, 7, 11, 12, 16, 18, 19, 20, 21, 27, 29, 31, 32, 33, 35, 36, 38, 39, 40, 41, 43, 44, 45, 46, 47, 48, 49, 51, 52, 53, 54, 55, 57, 58, 61, 63, 64, 65.	40	62
Total		65	-------

TABLE 11.—*Rhythmic unit [1] of song*

Songs containing—	Serial number of song	Number	Percent
No rhythmic unit	9, 15, 20, 24, 28, 35, 41, 64	8	12
One rhythmic unit	1, 2, 3, 4, 5, 6, 8, 10, 11, 14, 15, 17, 19, 21, 25, 27, 29, 30, 36, 37, 39, 40, 42, 49, 51, 53, 54, 57, 58, 62, 65.	31	48
Two rhythmic units	7, 12, 16, 18, 26, 31, 32, 33, 34, 43, 45, 55, 59, 60, 63	15	23
Three rhythmic units	4, 13, 22, 44, 46, 47, 48, 50, 52, 56	10	15
Four rhythmic units	61	1	2
Total		65	-------

[1] For the purpose of this analysis a rhythmic unit is defined as "a group of tones of various lengths, comprising more than one count of a measure, occurring more than twice in a song, and having an evident influence on the rhythm of the entire song."

TABLE 12.—*Rhythm (meter) of striking sticks used as an accompaniment to songs*

Rhythm of striking sticks	Serial number of song	Number	Percent
Eighth notes unaccented	62 (also 6 Duplicate)	1	2
Eighth notes accented in groups of two	58	1	2
Quarter notes unaccented	60, 61	2	2
Quarter notes, each beat preceded by an unaccented beat corresponding approximately to the third count of a triplet.	30, 40, 42, 43	4	6
Recorded without accompaniment		57	87
Total		65	-------

BIBLIOGRAPHY

BUSHNELL, DAVID I., JR.
1909. The Choctaw of Bayou Lacomb, St. Tammany Parish, Louisiana. Bur. Amer. Ethnol. Bull. 48.

CATLIN, GEORGE
1913. Illustrations of the manners and customs of the North American Indians. 2 vols. London.

CULIN, STEWART
1907. Games of the North American Indians. 24th Ann. Rep. Bur. Amer. Ethnol., 1902–03, pp. 1–846.

CUSHMAN, H. B.
1899. History of the Choctaw, Chickasaw and Natchez Indians.

DENSMORE, FRANCES
1910. Chippewa music. Bur. Amer. Ethnol. Bull. 45.
1913. Chippewa music—II. Bur. Amer. Ethnol. Bull. 53.
1918. Teton Sioux music. Bur. Amer. Ethnol. Bull. 61.
1922. Northern Ute music. Bur. Amer. Ethnol. Bull. 75.
1923. Mandan and Hidatsa music. Bur. Amer. Ethnol. Bull. 80.
1926. Music of the Tule Indians of Panama. Smithsonian Misc. Coll., vol. 77, No. 11.
1928. Uses of plants by the Chippewa Indians. 44th Ann. Rep. Bur. Amer. Ethnol. 1926–27, pp. 275–397.
1929. Chippewa customs. Bur. Amer. Ethnol. Bull. 86.
1929 a. Papago music. Bur. Amer. Ethnol. Bull. 90.
1929 b. Pawnee music. Bur. Amer. Ethnol. Bull. 93.
1932. Menominee music. Bur. Amer. Ethnol. Bull. 102.
1932 a. Yuman and Yaqui music. Bur. Amer. Ethnol. Bull. 110.
1936. Cheyenne and Arapaho music. Southwest Mus. Pap. No. 10. Los Angeles.
1937. The Alabama Indians and their music. In Straight Texas. Publ. Texas Folk-Lore Soc., No. 13, pp. 270–293.
1938. Music of Santo Domingo Pueblo, New Mexico. Southwest Mus. Pap. No. 12. Los Angeles.
1939. Nootka and Quileute music. Bur. Amer. Ethnol. Bull. 124.
1943. A search for songs among the Chitimacha Indians in Louisiana. Anthrop. Pap. No. 19, Bur. Amer. Ethnol. Bull. 133.

HELMHOLTZ, HERMANN LUDWIG FERDINAND VON
1885. On the sensations of tone as a physiological basis for the theory of music. Trans. by A. J. Ellis. 2d English ed. London.

HODGE, FREDERICK WEBB
1907. Handbook of American Indians north of Mexico, pt. 1. Bur. Amer. Ethnol. Bull. 30.

HOFER, MARI REUF
1907. Popular folk games and dances. A. Flanagan Co., Chicago.

ROYCE, CHARLES C.
1899. Indian land cessions in the United States. 18th Ann. Rep. Bur. Amer. Ethnol., 1896–97, pt. 2.

SWANTON, JOHN R.
1911. Indian tribes of the lower Mississippi Valley and adjacent coast of the Gulf of Mexico. Bur. Amer. Ethnol. Bull. 43.
1922. Early history of the Creek Indians and their neighbors. Bur. Amer. Ethnol. Bull. 73.
1931. Source material for the social and ceremonial life of the Choctaw Indians. Bur. Amer. Ethnol. Bull. 103.

2. MARY HICKMAN.

1. SIDNEY WESLEY.

2. OLMAN COMBY.

1. LYSANDER TUBBY.

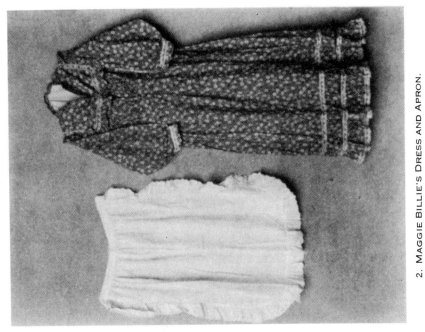

2. MAGGIE BILLIE'S DRESS AND APRON.

1. MAGGIE BILLIE IN NATIVE DRESS (1933).

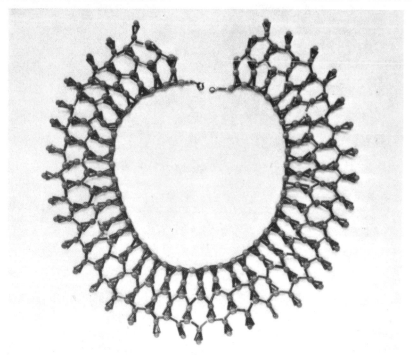

1. MAGGIE BILLIE'S BEAD COLLAR.

2. MAGGIE BILLIE'S FANCY COMB.

CHOCTAW CHILDREN IN NATIVE DRESS (1933).

1. MAN'S HEAD BAND OF PIERCED SILVER.

2. MAN'S BEAD COLLAR.

2. MARY HICKMAN'S HOUSE, WHERE SONGS WERE RECORDED.

1. ROBERT HENRY'S HOUSE, WHERE SONGS WERE RECORDED.

2. GROUP AT ROBERT HENRY'S HOUSE WHEN SONGS WERE RECORDED.

1. MAN'S BEAD NECKLACE.   2. RACKET USED IN BALL GAME.

3. SCRIMMAGE IN BALL GAME

BOB HENRY HOLDING RACKETS IN POSITION FOR PLAY.

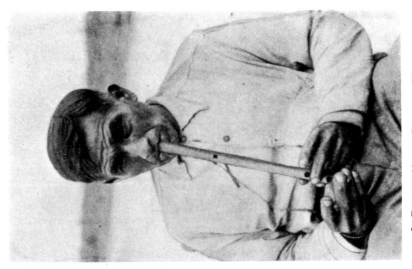

2. Robert Henry Blowing Whistle.

1. Whistle.

1. BALL USED IN BALL GAME

2. FOUR HANDKERCHIEFS FOLDED FOR USE IN BULLET GAME.